Who Took My Money?

Break Free from Debt Slavery

Monique Amyot

authorHOUSE®

AuthorHouse™
1663 Liberty Drive
Bloomington, IN 47403
www.authorhouse.com
Phone: 1-800-839-8640

First published by AuthorHouse 3/31/2009

ISBN: 978-1-4389-6854-4 (sc)

Printed in the United States of America
Bloomington, Indiana

This book is printed on acid-free paper.

What the people who have used the techniques in *Who Took My Money?* say:

"We greatly appreciated the good financial management techniques that you taught us. Even more, you gave us back our dreams. Your desire to pass on your knowledge to those who want to change poor spending habits and learn better money management is laudable. A wonderful mission!"

Marie Rose & Roch

"Monique revealed tools and important financial tricks to acquire the goals I most desired, including freedom from debt. Her teaching not only gave me the tools but also the motivation and hope to resume control of my personal financial state."

Cozette

"Last year, if someone would have told us we would be saving $425 more a month this year, thus removing all our financial stress, we wouldn't have believed it. We (now) have an excellent credit rating and always pay our bills on time. Thanks, Monique, for the precious advice and help."

Tasha

"My sincere thanks, Monique. I am a nurse who is the mother of 3 young children. My monthly payments are now $319 lower than they were with my bank. My house will be paid 4 years earlier. The valuable lesson from your course was just simply—phenomenal.

Marie-Sylvie

Who Took My Money

This publication is designed to provide accurate and authoritative information in regard to the subject matter covered. It is sold with the understanding that the publisher is not engaged in rendering legal, accounting, or other professional services. If legal advice or other expert assistance is required, the services of a competent professional should be sought.

Care has been taken to trace ownership of copyright material contained in this book; however, the publisher welcomes any information that enables it to rectify any reference or credit for subsequent editions.

Publisher: Partner Publishing

Editor: Karen Opas-Lanouette

Cover Design & Layout: Donald Lanouette

Illustrations: Camil Gravel, D. Lanouette

WHO TOOK MY MONEY

Printed in Canada

ISBN 978-0-9809925-0-2

1. Finance, Personal. 2. Financial Security 3. Self Help

Trade books are available at special quantity discounts to use for sales promotions, employee premiums, or educational purposes.

Please call our Special Sales Department to order or for more information at 1-866-553-7738, e-mail info@solutionfinance.ca, or write to: SolutionFinance, 4025-7 Innes Road, Ottawa, Ontario K1C 1T1

To learn more about ® Personal money management, please visit **www.solutionfinance.ca**

Acknowledgments

Great projects start with a dream and action, but without the help and support of many talented people *Who Took My Money* would never have seen the light of day. The list of the wonderful friends and family who made this book possible through their belief in me, encouragement, suggestions, and expertise is lengthy. From the bottom of my heart, **many** thanks.

To my wonderful children, Eliane, Karine, and Charles; my love goes out to you. You are more important to me than you could ever imagine. I offer my love and gratitude for their inspiration to my godchild Patrick and my brother Yvon, who have journeyed ahead of us to a better world.

Most of all, I am grateful to my parents who taught me that money could work for me or against me. I am now conscious that I have the choice between carrying the burden of debt slavery and financial worries or following some simple steps to become free to enjoy the life of my dreams.

Mom and Dad, thank you for the great gift you gave me by teaching the true value of money. I believe that your life story can help many achieve a happier, worry-free life.

To You, the Reader

This book can be a new beginning as you embark on your journey of self-discovery. In it, you will find key information that will lead to deeper and deeper levels of awareness in the game of life.

Your story could help someone else. Please share with me how this book has helped you and what changes you have made in your life.

I invite you to forward comments, questions, and personal experiences to our website at:

www.solutionfinance.ca or email: info@solutionfinance.ca

TABLE OF CONTENTS

TABLE OF CONTENTS

SECTION 1

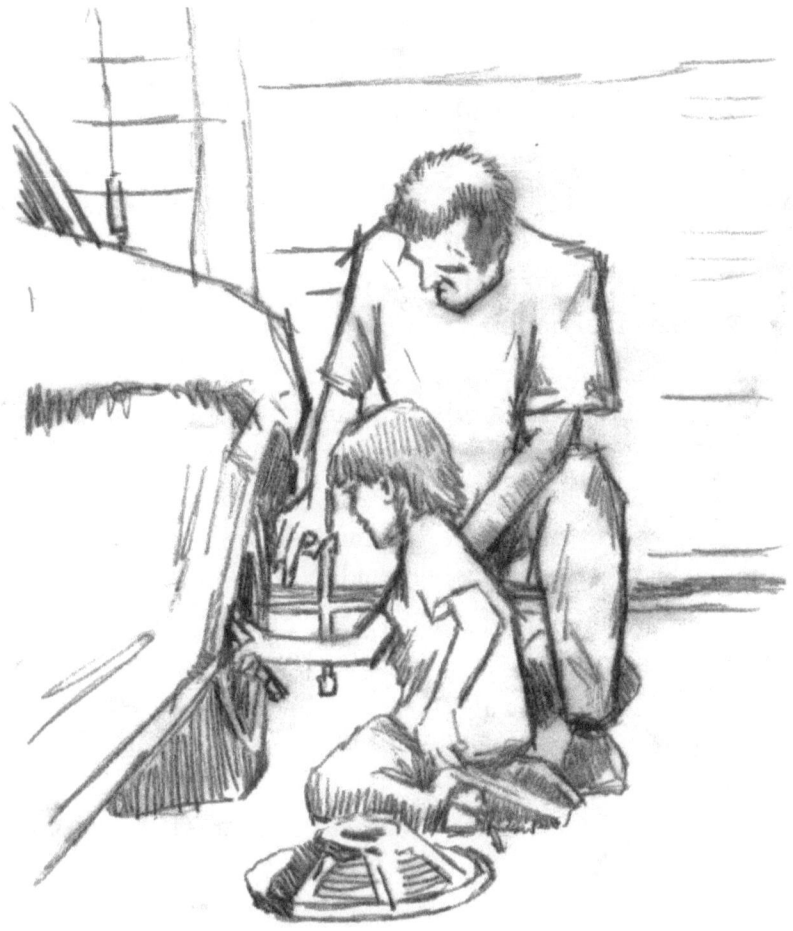

"There are two primary choices in life:
to accept conditions as they exist, or
accept the responsibility for changing them."
Denis Waitley

A Wise Man Shares his Financial Success

In my family we learned that managing money was simple and fun. My dad, whom we called "GP," said that the biggest problem in our world today is that people don't understand how money works, either through lack of knowledge, or by failing to take control.

GP's secrets are known to work by those who apply them. They teach how anyone can live a full and happy life.

GP taught us the rules of the game of life. To get ahead we were taught to pay ourselves first, instead of spending without thinking, or buying on impulse and then paying our creditors first!

Life wasn't easy for GP; he had to overcome many obstacles, but quitting was never an option for him.

A father of four daughters, one son, and 11 grandchildren, GP kept us together due to his strong family values. We grew up feeling loved and secure. Now, more than ever, I realize how grateful I am to have such wonderful parents.

GP taught us by example. He made a point of telling us that everything was possible. If we believed in our dreams, "NEVER quit!"

Our first requirement was to be very clear about what we really wanted and the price we'd have to pay to get it. To embrace this understanding as habit, my parents gave me a little fridge-magnet that said "You never fail until you stop trying." To this day, that message is proudly displayed on my fridge.

We were led to believe that financial education should be part of everyone's education and that it's never too late to start learning! GP's methods are proven to work for everyone brave enough to risk changing financial habits.

One thing I didn't know until recently is that GP taught my son Charles, among others, while repairing cars. Now GP is known as the mechanic with a self-taught MBA in financial planning. The family garage became an impromptu money management course for all who sought good money advice!

"Chains of habit are too light to be felt until they are too heavy to be broken." ~ Warren Buffett

Introduction

- Do you ever wonder where your hard earned money goes?
- Are you tired of feeling like you have been scammed, and don't know why or how?
- Do you wonder how to manage your finances efficiently?
- Would you like to use what you've got more effectively, but don't know where to start?

This book offers practical advice that is based on proven life experience. It shows how the average family, with children, a debt and making a modest income can take control of their financial lives. It's never too early or too late to embrace the road to financial health.

You will find keys to successfully navigate the money minefield. This is not a get rich quick plan, rather, this book will give you the tools to redefine your financial life in practical and manageable steps.

For ease of use, *Who Took My Money* is divided into three sections:

Section 1. Real life stories illustrating common financial situations.

Section II. Awareness, knowledge, and the Financial Tool Kit.

Section III. A practical 30 day plan to get you started.

The accompanying CD includes a variety of calculation tools and additional, pertinent information.

You have arrived at a crossroads; you're ready for a mind-over-money change.

A Wake-up Call

Many people are so busy working for money that they fail to take the time to really see where their money goes. This leads to a predictably disastrous financial future; one that destroys their cherished dreams.

We live in a culture that encourages us to spend now and worry about paying for it later. You can avoid the trap of financial slavery by applying GP's concepts and techniques.

Commitment to Change

Habits are not easily abandoned, and the best way to change them is to replace them. When you've suffered enough financial pain, you are likely to find ways and means to change your old thought processes and to forge new habits and behaviors. It takes courage and commitment to make these changes work. You must be prepared to win the battle of the mind before you can move on to the battle of the checkbook.

The value of a life is not only measured by the cost of a home or the material possessions accumulated over the years, it is also revealed by the satisfaction we experience in the way we use our time, our money, and our talents to impact our life and the lives of others.

Prologue

Life in the Family Garage

GP and his grandson Charles are singing as they work on Madame Fortier's car, having fun teasing each other. Charles, now 17 and with a hammer in hand, walks over to GP and says:

> "GP, I realize how lucky I am to have such a wonderful family. Not many of my friends have the privilege of having young grandparents who spend time with them. I love you grandpa, and I want you to know how grateful I am that you are teaching me about finances."

With tear-filled eyes, GP thought about his precious grandson and how he might guide Charles towards an easier life. GP had lived through some very difficult times, leading to the development of the wisdom that many saw in him.

GP: "You know, Charles, I believe that life should be fun. Time should be spent wisely. People end up on a treadmill of drudgery and toil, especially where money and freedom are concerned, because they are unwilling to take the few minutes a day to plan and manage. Instead, they wake up at night wondering how they will survive until the next paycheck."

Managing money is simple—so simple that most people don't believe in it and fail.

It takes only a few hours to set up a plan, and once done, you should never have to worry about running short of money again. You'll have the time and the means to do the things you enjoy with the people you love. I did it, and so can you."

Reaching into his pocketbook, GP took out an old, folded piece of paper and handed it to Charles, saying,

GP: "Live by these words and you will have more than you ever dreamed possible."

On it was written:

> ***Dream, Plan, Map, Adjust***
> *Rule #1: Pay Yourself First*

Charles wondered aloud when and how GP had become so good at managing money.

GP: "I'm sure your mom told you what she remembers, but she was pretty young when we went through the really tough times. I was born and raised on a farm, just finishing Grade 8 when my father died.

I moved to the city at 16 and, with my experience fixing farm machinery, got a job at a garage fixing cars. I soon found out that without a degree I would always just get by. I went back to school to get a mechanic's license.

For some reason, I always believed in saving a bit of money, even though I liked a good time on the weekends. By the time I was 25, I was able to scrape together enough money to take over a failing gas station. I fixed cars and your grandmother looked after the pumps."

Charles: "Why don't you have that gas station anymore?"

GP: "Well, I forgot something pretty important. We made a success out of someone else's failed business. Because I was nervous, had a bit of self-doubt, and wanted an out, I only signed a two year lease. When it expired, we were faced with a huge rent increase. I hadn't taken into consideration that if we succeeded our landlord would take advantage of us. That was one of life's most difficult lessons. I didn't believe enough in myself to fully accept that we would succeed and I paid for that lesson by losing my place of business. I walked away from it. I still dreamed of having my own business and so I went into business with a friend doing demolitions."

Charles: "But you don't have a demolition business any more, GP."

GP: "Life doesn't always go the way you plan it! I was dumping sand to make a beach in front of the cottage when one of my dump-trucks collapsed on me. My ribs were broken, my spleen was crushed, and I suffered a whole bunch of other injuries. In fact, when I was brought to the hospital, the doctors figured I wouldn't make it. As you can see, I survived. But they told me I'd never work again. It was a very bad time for your grandmother and me.

I couldn't work for almost two years. Between five young kids and the care I needed, your grandmother couldn't leave the house to work, so we had no income. What kept us from going under was the fact we had no debts, no mortgage on our modest home, and our car was paid for. We had always saved part of our income, no matter how small, so we had a small emergency fund.

The kids never knew just how bad things were for us. We managed to have enough fun without spending money. This was when I fully understood that debt compounded life's difficulties and realized 'Never commit to needless debt.'"

Charles: "So, after learning the first rule of paying yourself first, you simply added rule number two—avoid needless debt!"

GP: "You got it! When I was well enough to go back to work, I decided I could best provide for my family's needs through a steady income and I spent the rest of my working life at the cement company. That way, I had the means to take advantage of opportunities when they presented themselves.

I worked at an 'ordinary' job, at an average wage. But guess what? Life presented me with good opportunities along the way and, having followed the Golden rule, I manage to set aside enough savings so that I could both benefit from sudden opportunities and cope with the unexpected. We always saved for the 'toys' we wanted and I don't go into debt unless it is totally purposeful and I can see how to manage it without risking our family's security.

Over the years, even a few dollars a week multiplied into something big. And that's why grandma and I can afford to travel for three or four months a year, buy a new car without borrowing, and enjoy life without worrying about money. You know that in our family we respect money and plan for the future by saving for our dreams."

The Desire to Change

To those who have Dreams and are willing to:

- Set GOALS to achieve them
- Create a vision PLAN
- Learn DISCIPLINE and WILL POWER
- Practice to PERFECT
- Persist to WIN!

"To the ones who see FAR, there's nothing IMPOSSIBLE"
~ Henry Ford

Hard Lessons

Money Traps & Pitfalls

In the following stories you will learn why and how it's easy to be taken advantage of by a system that is designed to keep you in a prison of debt because it benefits the lender.

We're told that not only do we deserve the best; we can afford it— even if we don't have the money in the bank! Money constantly goes out quicker than it comes in. We are told that we need to spend money to have fun. This simply isn't true.

How do you stop believing in the myths and prevent marketers from picking your pocket?

There are many ways that a person can be taken advantage of every day and this only ensures that they will remain at the bottom of the ladder longer.

Do you recognize a pitfall when you see one?

- Buy now, pay later.
- Payday loans; cash advances to handle emergencies until payday. (Evidence of poor money management.)
- Debt consolidation loans.
- Rent to own.
- Taking money from your home equity to consolidate debts.

Fraud

When it's too Good to be True

Elaine, a teacher in her late 40's, attended an investment seminar that was presented by Edward, a well-liked and trusted member of Elaine's church. Edward spoke knowledgably about investments and offered a guaranteed, no risk return of 15% from a fund he managed. Other members of the church who had invested with him praised his financial acumen. The opportunity to retire five years earlier than planned, the no-risk factor, and the good rate of return all made it seem like a golden opportunity, so Elaine invested her retirement savings of $180,000 in Edward's fund.

A few years later a friend convinced her that something was wrong—she had received no annual reports—and Elaine told Edward that she would like to withdraw her money. He said that he could give her $5,000 right away, but would need time to liquidate the stocks to give her the rest. This kept up for sometime until Elaine finally took Edward to court. It soon became obvious that Edward's investment fund was fraudulent. The police calculated that Edward stole over 4 million dollars from the people who had entrusted him with their money. Only a few lucky "seed" customers at the start of his scheme got their money back.

Elaine didn't think she was being greedy—15% didn't seem like an outrageous rate of return. She felt that Edward was trustworthy because he was a member of her church and was recommended by people she respected. He relied on that mindset to find his victims. If something seems a little too good to be true, it usually is! A quick check would have revealed that there isn't a single legitimate investment that GUARANTEES a 15% rate of return. Beware of any investment opportunity that uses the following phrases:

- Guaranteed profit.
- No risk.
- Get in on the ground floor.
- Offer available for a limited time only.
- I'll get you the paperwork later.
- Just make your check out to me, personally.

Scammed Out of a Down Payment
Isabelle is a single mom of three living on one income. After living in a mobile home for 10 years, she was very excited to find a reputable home builder who was willing to give her a loan, one with great terms. She made a $3,000 deposit.

About two weeks before the house was ready to close, the builder's agent called and said they needed an additional $1,000 down payment so that Isabelle could qualify for the loan. They called her the day after her mom went into the hospital for emergency surgery, so she was distracted. Isabel met the agent late in the evening, paid the $1,000, and signed the paper agreeing to the new down payment amount, even though it wiped out her bank account.

What she didn't realize was that, by signing the new paperwork, she agreed to forfeit her original deposit of $3,000 if she was unable to buy the house for ANY reason. One week later, the builder's agent informed Isabelle that she no longer qualified for the loan and that she couldn't have her $3,000 deposit back.

It was three weeks before Christmas and Isabelle and her family were left with nowhere to live. She couldn't even afford a hotel room because she had wiped out her emergency fund to pay the additional $1,000. Isabelle, who thought that she could trust a reputable builder, states simply, "I felt so stupid."

Should you Loan Money to Friends or Family Members?
An Expensive Truck

Paul went to see his favorite grandfather to ask him to co-sign on a loan. He wanted to buy a brand new truck with a price tag of $35,000. He said he needed it for work. His grandfather decided to make Paul a personal loan with a 5% rate of return, far better than anything that the bank or car-dealership would give him.

Paul promised to repay grandfather $500 a month until the loan was fully paid. The first month passed and no payment was made. The next month Paul lost his job and had no way of repaying his grandfather. Months passed and Paul hadn't made a single payment. His grandfather decided that Paul had to sell the truck to repay his debt. The truck sold for $28,000, leaving Grandfather short by $7,000 and very angry at his grandson.

What do you think happened to this previously close relationship?

- How do you think the grandfather felt?
- How do you think the grandson felt?

The Thoughtless Newly Weds

Luc was happy to lend his son and future daughter-in-law $15,000 to buy their first home, as the couple had saved no money towards a down payment. The couple then had a lavish wedding and received a substantial amount of money as gifts. Only six months after returning from their honeymoon abroad, the couple decided to take a trip to

Cancun. At this point, it had been nine months since Luc had lent his son $15,000 and not a penny had been repaid.

At the next Sunday dinner the new wife and her mother-in-law were discussing where to shop in Cancun. Luc and his son, sitting a little further away, caught the conversation and looked at each other. The son, suddenly ashamed, turned his head away and said nothing. The uncomfortable silence continued for a long time.

- How do you think the father felt?
- How do you think the son felt?

Till Debt do Us Part
Sean learned that lending money to a friend can be a quick way to lose a friendship. When a friend failed to pay back a loan, Sean thought about it and decided that the friendship was worth more than any amount of money. Sean called Mike to tell him that he owed nothing and that Sean wanted to return the friendship to its old footing, but Mike was never comfortable with Sean again and the relationship faded away.

When it comes to family and friends, do not loan—GIVE. Then you get the joy of giving and receiving. When you make a loan, you are no longer equals in the relationship and it is easy for resentments to spring up.

Get it in Writing
The Broken Nest—She Trusted a Verbal Agreement
Pearl married young and, for 24 years, life was wonderful. She and her husband had three great kids and, by managing their money, had ended up with a nice home in a great neighborhood with only a few thousand dollars left to pay on the mortgage. Life consisted of a lot of laughter, love, and contained no money worries. And then it all fell apart.

Pearl moved out of her home with just a few pieces of furniture and her personal belongings. She and her husband made a verbal agreement; everything they had jointly worked for would be given to their children.

Six years later, Pearl received a legal notice that her husband owed her nothing and he was now the sole owner of the family home. Pearl sought legal advice only to discover that one cannot claim marital rights after six years of separation. It was too late; the verbal agreement she had trusted him to keep was not respected. Everything she had worked hard for was gone, and there was no way to get it back.

Peal learned the hard way that you have to know your rights and act to protect them without delay when challenged. In retrospect, she should have consulted a lawyer who specialized in marital disputes and understood the laws and their financial implications. But at the time, Pearl worried that doing so might make things with her ex more hostile and hence tougher on the kids. Pearl learned a tough lesson—get it in writing!

Windfalls Rarely Solve Money Problems
Man Wins $24 Million Dollars in Lottery & Ends Up Bankrupt
John, a former nurse who won $24 million dollars in a lottery, ended up bankrupt with over $5 million in debt and all of his possessions seized. He currently lives in subsidized social housing. At the time he won the lottery he was broke and sleeping on an air mattress in his mother's apartment.

John spent lavishly from the start. He bought fancy cars, made generous gifts to charities, and purchased a mansion. Fulfilling many men's dreams, he invested in a sports team. Rather than making him money, the team ended up costing him millions. John's dream jackpot win became a nightmare.

It's not winning a jackpot that solves money problems, it's whether you understand money management. You'll make the same errors on the large scale as you make on the small scale, if you don't change your attitude towards money and how you handle it. For John (and many other lottery winners), the same habits and attitudes that put them in financial trouble before they won the lottery eventually brought them right back to poverty, debt, and worry, despite their windfall win.

Little Changes Can Make a Big Difference
An Early Retirement
Terry was 50 when he retired from his job as a civil service engineer. He was the only one of his fellow engineers able to do this (and maintain the

same standard of living as if he was working). When his coworkers asked him how he did it, this was his response:

"It's simple. When you guys headed out to buy a donut and a coffee for a mid-morning snack, I enjoyed an apple from home and coffee from the office coffee pot at 50 cents a cup.

At lunch time, I didn't go out for a pizza slice or submarine sandwich; I brought my lunch from home. And on Monday mornings, when we chatted about what we had done that weekend, most of you had eaten a few meals out. My wife and I kept that for special occasions.

Did you ever try and figure out ALL the money you spent at restaurants and coffee shops—just at work, even?

- Donut and ordinary coffee (twice a day) = $4
- Cheap lunch = $7

These little changes added up to an extra $2,600 a year to put into investments. Now calculate how much that adds up to over 30 years—and don't forget compound interest! And that's how I was able to retire 15 years earlier than most."

Not Planning for the Inevitable
Tragedy Strikes Unexpectedly

Olivia married the man of her dreams when she was only 19. For over 20 years they blissfully lived the American dream; a new home, two cars, and frequent vacations. She was a typical housewife with three kids, while he took care of the money. The family never lacked for anything.

Then tragedy struck! Without any warning, Olivia's husband dropped dead at work from a heart attack. Their savings barely covered the funeral expenses. The bills began to pile up. She was grief stricken, barely able to function, and, at the best of times, had no idea of budgeting. Olivia didn't even have the passwords to the majority of the family's bank accounts. Creditors called almost every day, threatening legal action.

She discovered that they had no life insurance and was soon forced to sell the house. Luckily, there was enough equity built up in it that Olivia was able to get a much smaller apartment and pay to take a course in basic secretarial skills so that she could get a job. Now, after several hard years, she has decent savings, proper insurance, and a company medical plan that handles just about every health concern, including dental.

Through tragedy, Olivia learned that it is important to hope for the best, but prepare for the worst.

Find more stories and information on the accompanying CD.

WHO TOOK MY MONEY?

Put simply—NO ONE TOOK YOUR MONEY!

The choices you make about finances:
- Being poor is a choice.
- Being middle class is a choice.
- Being rich is a choice.

The beliefs you have about money:
- I am worthy of my money.
- I believe that wealthy people are good, honest and caring.
- I will make as much money as my heart desires.

The respect you give money:
- Take good care of it and it will last MUCH longer.
- Take time to DREAM - PLAN – MAP – ADJUST.
- Create a system that works for you.

KNOWLEDGE + WILL = POWER

The Importance of Self-talk

What we say to ourselves in our innermost thoughts reflects our core beliefs, which influence our attitudes and behaviour.

Core beliefs don't necessarily reflect truth and are influenced by parents, teachers, family, and friends. They are rarely challenged and limit us from reaching our potential. Other false core-beliefs arise from traumatic emotional, financial, or relationship-related experiences where we simply reacted out of a need for self-preservation, resulting in a knee-jerk reaction to all such future events.

We end up living the present where, programmed by past fears, we create a similar future.

Questioning our core beliefs is a major step in regaining control of all aspects of life, including finances. All forms of personal freedom (physical, mental, emotional, spiritual, and financial) begin with this process.

Language Creates Reality

Mastering the language you use to describe your reality is important. It affects your overall perspectives and reinforces your attitudes about money, whether negative or positive.

What seems like more fun; *spending* or *saving* money? Most people will choose spending. So, since spending is what we prefer to do, see what happens when you think about your money in terms of *spending* less, rather than *saving* more.

"I always run out of money before the end of the month."

This is a classic misuse of the power of the spoken word. In this case, a negative and self-limiting reality is created and reinforces the speaker's core belief that he or she is powerless to make choices about how money is used.

Our choice of words is important.

To change our thinking and to open up a new perspective in money use, try the following language strategy. Consider every financial transaction (without exception) an ***investment***, either wise or foolish.

Now, let's see if languaging our money-use strategies and applications reflects sound and healthy perspectives:

- I choose to **invest** money in a case of whiskey and intend to consume it within the next week. This is obviously a poor investment since the results will likely lead to any of many negative outcomes.

- I choose to **invest** money in going to see a movie with my family or friends. The proper use of money in this case leads to at least the potential of enjoyment—a sound investment!

Try framing some of your current money transactions in this language. It will help create an awareness of some of the unconscious beliefs and habits that can lead to so much money stress.

These are the 7 golden rules of finance!

Facilitate your financial education.

Initiate a new way of thinking.

Never live above your means.

Apply the basic financial principles.

Never forget to pay yourself first.

Come to know the magic of compound interest.

Eliminate bad debt.

SECTION TWO

The Path to a Happier Life

For many people, money issues have become a nightmare.

We live in a society of unnecessary consumerism, driven by mass-media hype to have it all now. We fail to see the terrible price we pay for quick gratification.

The "must have" mentality of today's society will only stop when we realize that we have become slaves to big business and others who benefit from our suffering. We are literally mortgaging our lives into debt slavery.

Just a few easy steps are all it takes to be in control. If you choose to let your money manage itself, you will wake up one day wondering, "WHO TOOK MY MONEY?"

My sincere wish is that you put into practice the techniques described in the following pages. Respect your money and treat it as a friend. It will make a tremendous difference in your life and the lives of your loved ones.

I dedicate this book to those willing to follow their dreams, with the courage to change their money habits and create an action plan. Make the decision to walk the path of self-determination and you win at the game of life.

This power is in YOU to fulfill your dreams!

Chapter 1

NAVIGATING THE MONEY MINEFIELD

"The difference between great people and everyone else is that great people create their lives actively, while everyone else is created by their lives, passively waiting to see where life takes them next. The difference between the two is the difference between living fully and just existing."
Michael E. Gerber

"No man's credit is as good as his money." ~ John Dewey

GP: "Money looks after us when we look after our money. But all you need to do is have a look at the statistics to see that more and more people are getting into money trouble. It makes me sad, because I KNOW that they are losing the most precious thing we have, time to enjoy our loved ones and favourite activities, to worry and stress over their bills."

Many people stumble aimlessly in a financial minefield, programmed to repeat painful experiences until they realize that there must be a better way. Most never escape the vicious cycles of poverty and deprivation because they were never taught the fundamentals of money management. In their ignorance, they never come to realize just how important money management skills are until sudden crisis or prolonged difficulties arise and they are forced to learn or fall into financial chaos.

STATISTICS

If you feel a little embarrassed by your money habits, here are a few statistics that show that you are not alone:

- 70% of North Americans live paycheck to paycheck.
- Most Canadians pay more annual interest on debt than a family of four spends on groceries over the same year.
- In 1976, 10,000 Canadians filed for personal bankruptcy but, by 2007, that number had climbed to 108,830. In the same year, bankruptcies in the USA amounted to 850,912.
- According to The Canadian Bankruptcy institute, 69% of filers blame credit-card debt for their insolvency.
- Astonishingly, 89% of bankrupts still get offered a new credit card.
- Canadians currently owe more than $458 billion in debt. That's almost $15,000 for each Canadian.
- In the USA, the national debt currently runs at over $7.2 trillion.
- 78% of people that consolidate debt (mainly credit cards) owe even more than their consolidation in less than a year.

FACTS

Do you recognize yourself in any of the following statements? If so, part of you probably thinks that you have no power over money. But it is never too late! All you need to do is take a few simple steps and you'll discover that, no matter the size of your income, you have enough money for all of your needs and many of your wants:

- I am powerless to manage money. No one is powerless.
- Don't blame me; my parents always fought over money. 90% of people with financial difficulties habitually make excuses, blaming parents, teachers, and even financial institutions for not teaching them how to manage money.
- I tried budgeting and quit because things always came up unexpectedly. Few people are taught healthy money habits, but everyone can choose to change their habits and learn new money skills.
- I always run out of money before month's end. Incomes are inadequate to lifestyles, so it's our choice of lifestyle that has to change.
- I'm not going to worry about money today; it will all work out okay. People want to be wealthy and healthy without effort. Life doesn't work that way.
- I'm so far behind in my bills that I think it is hopeless for me. Personal debt-loads are dangerously high, affecting many from every walk of life and income.
- My spouse left me because of the constant stress and fights over meeting our payments. Money worries impact our relationships, activities, and our ability to realize cherished dreams.
- My job is boring drudgery, but I know I'll never get fired. Most employees stay in jobs they hate because they mistakenly believe they have financial security.
- If only I had more money, I'd be happy. Happiness is a decision. It does not depend on accumulating possessions, nor is it the result of a hefty bank-balance.

MYTHS

There are many myths about money that, if we believe them, hold us back from achieving real wealth. Some of the most common are:

- Money is the source of all evil.

- Money can't buy you happiness.

- Debt is a good tool for creating prosperity. The truth is that debt adds enormous risk factors to life and, although some succeed, most new businesses will fail in the first year, consuming the investor's life savings.

- Most people think that with time, their money problems will go away. The truth is that as long as they do nothing, they will GET WORSE.

- To become wealthy, you just need to learn how to buy investment property with "no money down." The truth is that many people who follow this route to wealth often end up losing their shirts.

- The poor are poor because of their upbringing and where they grew up. In some parts of the world it may take a truly exceptional person to rise out of poverty, but no one in North America has that excuse to fall back on. Here, poverty is created by the choices we make. The problem is that we don't *know* we have choices.

- Money is not for me. Some people believe they don't deserve to be wealthy or that there is only so much of the pie to go around. Creating wealth and financial freedom is available to everyone and not only is it is our birth-right, it's our duty, offering the means to contribute.

- It's a man's world. He brings home the bacon, so he has the right to control the money. This attitude can create all sorts of problems. For starters, the spouse who earns the most money may not have great money skills. A bigger paycheck may just equal a bigger debt load. The spouse who backs away from money management on these grounds backs away from a major adult responsibility. Healthy couples communicate about money and regularly review their finances and goals together.

The Biggest Myth of All; Money is Difficult to Manage

Do you remember learning how to walk? No? Next time you are around toddlers, watch them closely. They totter around, lose their balance unexpectedly, fall over in all directions, and often get some painful bumps and bruises. But they still keep trying, even through the tears, until they master the skill of walking.

A few years later, they do exactly the same when they learn how to read. Painstaking, repetitive effort is rewarded by the thrilling ability to read a story without having to wait for a "grown-up" to find the time. Acquiring the skill of managing your money takes nothing that you don't *already* have. You proved it all those years ago when you learned how to walk, talk, and read.

Just because you didn't learn the skill of financial management (yet), it doesn't stop you from starting the process today! Like any new ability, the early days require a bit more effort and time commitment. It will soon become so routine that the effort involved is barely noticeable. The same can't be said for the results. Your bank accounts will be healthy, bills will no longer be a stress point, and credit cards will barely feature in your life, as you'll have the hard cash to purchase the items that you truly want.

A LITTLE INSPIRATION

THE LITTLE BOY AND LUCK

A tired little boy lay down to rest at the edge of a deep well. As he slept, he rolled over until he was only an inch away from falling in. The goddess Luck appeared beside him. She said, "Little boy, please wake up. If you fall into the well, I will be blamed for your death, for I find that humans always blame their disasters on me, however much they are caused by their own actions."

Chapter 2

WHAT IS MONEY?

"Everyone is more or less the master of his own fate."
Aesop

"Money is neither my god nor my devil. It is a form of energy that tends to make us more of who we already are, whether it's greedy or loving." ~ Dan Millman

GP: "Charles, have you ever wondered why it is that so many people today have money problems that create all sorts of stress for themselves and their family? The truth is that the real problem is NOT money, but rather how a person's perception, knowledge, values, and behavior align with the laws of money."

Money as a Tool

Money should not be your master; it is there to serve you.

Money is a tool. Used with a little care, it not only makes sure our basic needs are met, it also provides security for our loved ones and the freedom to indulge our wants without worry. There is no reason for money (or lack of it) to be a cause of anxiety, as it is for so many people.

Money comes in many forms; paper dollars, metal coins or virtual credit (even tobacco has been used as money). Any asset that can be exchanged for value can be used as money. A common mistake is to think that money will fix all that ails us. For example, lottery winners are often so excited when they win a large amount that they spend without thought or limits until they hit bottom. The thought of saving or meaningful investment escapes them, and they find themselves worse off than before their big win.

5 Laws about Money

1 People first—then money.
2 Look at what you have—not at what you had.
3 Money flows—in the direction of the intention of its director.
4 The truth creates money—lies will destroy it.
5 Money is a tool—it has no power of its own.

On CD: The 13 Laws of Prosperity.

NUTS AND BOLTS

Remember: **money is a tool** and you are the one who wields it. A hammer can build a house or destroy it. You are the one who holds the "money" hammer! Use it wisely and enjoy the results. Ask yourself:

What does money mean to me?
What do I truly want from my financial future?
What does having enough money mean?
What fears do I have related to money?

DAVIE'S MONEY TREE

One day, little Davie found a rare, special seed. He showed it to his father who told him he was the lucky owner of a Money Tree seed and then helped him to plant it. Davie started reading stories about Money Trees and their care. His research showed that in the early years a Money Tree needs a lot of tending and has only a slim chance of reaching maturity. Davie had to spend time with his baby tree every day and water it regularly. At first it grew so slowly that he could hardly notice any difference, no matter how much care he gave it. And then a year later some optimistic signs appeared. The tree produced a few leaves that turned out to be dollar bills. The next year it produced more leaves. With each year of care, the Money Tree produced more and more money, until it was able to look after all of Davie's needs, as long as he also looked after his tree.

Chapter 3

A WEALTHY MINDSET

"Wealth is not a material gain, but a state of mind."
Jerry Gillies

"Too many people spend money they haven't earned, to buy things they don't want, to impress people they don't like." ~ Will Rogers

GP: "I read a lot of stories by and about millionaires. I think they are a lot like tree surgeons who cut away the barren branches that steal sap from the fruit-bearing branches. By pruning away the habits of impulsive spending, I learned very quickly that money set aside, even in small amounts, grows as magically as any Money Tree. The millionaires' stories also showed me that cutting unnecessary expenditures meant that, at the right moment, I could harvest enough to have whatever I desired.

From a young age, I have practiced pruning my money tree and now I enjoy a good income from my investments. Because of this, lack of money never limits my enjoyment of life. I suggest you begin now, by treating the money you would otherwise spend on treats like a seed. Wait until the right moment when you'll find an opportunity to make it grow. That's called investing. As it matures and is nurtured correctly, you'll find that $20 and $50 bills are ripe for the picking once your investments hit the 5 year mark."

The Rich Mindset

Everyone dreams of being wealthy. The truth is that wealthy people have a certain mindset and apply certain principles that others don't. If you want to be wealthy, apply the same principles as the rich. Surveys show that, unlike the majority who live paycheck to paycheck, millionaires don't drive new cars, nor do they wear the latest fashions, or buy the latest accessories. Their homes rarely reflect their financial status.

Rich people create their fortunes by combining saving and investing. They have a plan and discipline themselves to follow it. The average millionaire knows exactly how much money he has and what it's doing, always.

"Rich" isn't just a dollar value. It's having the time and means to enjoy the activities and people who make you happy. It's a mindset you achieve once your dreams and your money management line up.

GP: *"Money can't buy happiness, but it certainly can afford us a better style of misery!"*

Seriously, we all know that money doesn't make us happy, but deep down inside (secretly) we believe it will. What we fail to realize is that even if a million dollars did land in our bank account, it wouldn't take long before we'd be just as stressed with money worries as before, thanks to keeping the same habits that got us into trouble in the first place.

The Illusion of Wealth: Danger Signals

Every day, we see hundreds of images and messages that tell us that the right product will make us sexier, smarter, more likeable, respected, admired, feared, envied, and so forth. The lifestyles of the rich and famous are thrust in our faces, so that we know more about their mansions than we do about the majority of our neighbours' houses.

It's a rare person who hasn't momentarily felt the thrill of what it would be like to be rich when throwing down a credit card for a high-end purchase that is far beyond their budget. Regularly giving in to this sensation can create serious financial damage. People rack up huge debt and ultimately lose their homes and savings to this seductive addiction.

Do you or your spouse:
- Buy brand new furniture on credit when the old things are just fine, except that they aren't stylish enough to reflect your desired self-image?
- Justify buying expensive clothes for professional reasons when, in reality, they are far more expensive than what everyone else at work (including the boss) is wearing?
- Always insist on picking up the tab for meals and drinks when you are out with friends or work colleagues, even though you don't have money in the bank to pay for it?

From Rags to Riches

Over the past thirty-five years, the multi-billionaire Warren Buffett has emerged as arguably the greatest investor in American history. If you had invested $10,000 in Berkshire Hathaway when he took control in 1965, your holdings would be worth more than $50 million today. The second-richest man in the world, Buffett still lives in the same house he bought three decades ago for $31,500, drives an older Lincoln Town car, and downs countless cans of Coca-Cola every day.

GP: "I didn't have much more then the basic needs when I grew up. I wanted a life where I didn't worry about the bills coming due and whether I could ever afford to retire. I came to understand that I had to observe and follow what the rich did, so that I could one day have the prosperity that I wanted."

What Wealthy People Share in Common

- They live well below their means.
- They allocate their time, energy, and money efficiently, in ways conducive to building wealth.
- They believe that financial independence is more important than displaying high social status.
- Their parents did not provide economic help.
- Their adult children are economically self-sufficient.
- They are skilled in targeting market opportunities.
- They chose the right occupations.

Millionaires' Money Habits

Building a real-life money tree is a great way to boost your earnings and build your financial freedom. Your goal at the end will be the very fruitful reward of thousands of dollars. Who said money doesn't grow on trees? In order to become wealthy, you need to put aside some of your income into something that will create more money and compound over time. You might want to strive to save more. For one, the more you invest, the more money you'll have and the faster you'll reach your financial goals. But there's more to it than just the speed at which you create your wealth. There are some very important issues that need to be considered as you map out your financial plan.

NUTS AND BOLTS

The rich have only **ONE** secret: they do **NOT ACQUIRE DEBT EXCEPT FOR AN ECONOMICALLY BENEFICIAL PURPOSE—** they make interest work for them, NOT for the Bank.

A LITTLE INSPIRATION

"WANTS NOW!" - A CAUTIONARY TALE

Sara and John stopped off at a big box store to buy printer ink. On the way to the ink cartridges, they walked by a giant plasma TV at 30% off the regular price. It had great sound, HD, and was sexy enough to wow their friends on game night. Instead of meeting their original goal to save money on printer ink, they walked out having spent an extra $1,899 (plus tax).

The new TV looked a little too good in their family room, so they decided to renovate the room and turn it into a home theatre. Sara and John figured it was a good investment, as they'd spend less money going out. Of course, they did need to install new lighting, sound proof the room, put in a new floor, buy a great sound system (wireless), and get some new seating. Just for fun, they put in an old style popcorn cart, too. All these purchases were made on credit.

John and Sara's original need for a printer cartridge ($50) turned into a spiral of costly wants (over $23,000 + interest) that they will be paying for long after their teenage son has finished university.

Chapter 4

MODERN SLAVERY

"Modern man drives a dealer-financed car over a bond-financed highway on credit card gas."

Earl Wilson

> *"You want to make 21% returns risk free?*
> *Pay off your credit cards."* ~ Earl Wilson

The dictionary defines debt as an obligation by one individual or company to pay a specific amount of money to another party.

According to the web site *Motley Fool*, the average North-American is carrying **$8,562** in credit card debt. Whew! That's a lot of chains!

Debt Steals Your Tomorrows by Enslaving You to Your Yesterdays

Most people with debt problems are so caught up in their Lifestyle Cycle or their debt juggling that they can't imagine finding a positive solution. They remain paralyzed by their circumstances. Though they would be grateful to end the ongoing stress of debt, they seldom evolve their thinking enough to escape this self-imposed prison.

It is almost impossible to move forward when a large portion of your income is used to repay the interest on your credit cards. Just imagine how much more you could buy if you didn't have to pay so much interest.

GP: "Charles, if you go to the book store you will see hundreds of new books on finance, so why is it that so many people live in debt and from paycheck to paycheck, no matter their income or profession?

A big part is that people today buy into the idea that there is such a thing as good debt. I think consumer debt is a form of slavery. Every day, marketers tell you that you MUST have this new toy, that this is the best sale ever! And the businesses make it easy with no-money-down credit plans. What makes you think you will have that money in 6 months, or even 18 months, if you don't have it today?"

Hundreds of advertisements every day are aimed at convincing you that you need some product you've obviously managed quite well without until now. When you're hit with the same message often enough, it can override your logic. Advertisers and marketers count on constant repetition of their ads or slogans to drive the message home.

A great deal of sophisticated marketing is designed to make us believe we are entitled to live an affluent lifestyle that takes major cash outlay to maintain. Even if we manage to keep up appearances for a while, our whole lifestyle can collapse when the debt load becomes too heavy for the crumbling foundation of poorly managed finances.

Credit Danger Signals

If you find yourself using the following strategies to make purchases, you are at risk of excessive debt (if you aren't there already):
- Don't pay a cent until…
- No interest, no payments, for 1 full year.
- Use your credit card and save 10%.
- Buy here and we'll give you air miles.

Ever wonder what it really costs to make a purchase on your credit card?
- The average person who buys with a credit card rather than cash ends up paying as much as 23% more for the item by the time they've finally paid off the bill.

Fact
- Debt is now at 109% of the average annual net income.
- In 70% of divorces, the number one factor that contributed to the divorce was arguing about money.

What these statistics *don't* show is the painful worry that affects the happiness and health of people carrying unmanageable debt loads.

The Black Beast of Credit Debt

> *"No man's credit is as good as his money."* ~ John Dewey

Credit cards are the *bête noir* of personal finance. The more you use them, the worse your money situation gets.

GP: "The list of misconceptions about credit cards is so long that we could spend all night talking about them. Most people don't realize that by using a credit card they are actually taking out a loan. If the money they borrowed is repaid within the `forgive' period (which is getting shorter and shorter), no interest is paid. If you don't pay the loan off entirely, you pay a MUCH higher interest rate than you would with any other form of loan.

And don't get me started on air miles and reward points; the high interest rate and fees these cards come with mean that your kitchen gadget or flight (when you can book one!) ends up being pricier than if you hadn't put all that debt onto your credit card. Remember, there's no such thing as a free lunch, my boy."

Younger and Younger
More than 89% of today's graduating students have credit card debt even before they have a job, thanks to heavy marketing of student credit cards.

Debt Consolidation
Debt consolidation can be another trap. It seems like a solution, but there are two problems:
* Most people who take out consolidation loans don't put in the effort to change their money habits and end up in even more debt.
* Most people don't grasp that the extended payback period of the consolidation loan means that, even though the monthly payment is lower, they end up paying more interest to the lender. This method is a short term feel-good solution that usually creates long term problems.

The Secrets that Credit Card Companies Don't Want
You to Know (Adapted from Military.com)
Interest Backdating. If you are carrying any balance from previous months, interest is charged on all new purchases without a grace period. Increasingly, companies now charge you interest from the day of the actual purchase, rather than the day that they pay the store.

Remedy: Find another card issuer, or always pay your bill in full by the due date.

Two-Cycle Billing. Issuers, who use this method of calculating interest, charge two months worth of interest for the first month you failed to pay off your total balance in full. This issue arises only when you switch from paying in full to carrying a balance from month to month.

Remedy: Switch issuers or always pay your balance in full.

The Right to Setoff. If you have money on deposit at a bank, and also have your credit card there, you may have signed an agreement when you opened the deposit account which permits the bank to take those funds if you become delinquent on your credit card.

Remedy: Bank at separate institutions, or avoid delinquencies.

Interest Rate Hikes Are Retroactive. If you sign up for a credit card with a low "teaser" rate, such as 7.9%, when the low rate period expires, your existing balance will likely be subject to the regular and substantially higher interest rate.

Remedy: Pay in full before the rate increase or close the account.

Shortened Due Dates. Most card issuers offer a 25 day grace period in which to pay for new purchases without incurring finance charges. Some banks have shortened the grace period to 20 days—but only for customers who pay in full monthly.

Remedy: Ask to go back to 25 days.

Eliminating Grace Periods. That fabulous offer you received in the mail for a gold card with a $10,000 credit limit, and lots of features may not be so great. The most common "string" attached is that the card has no grace period. You are charged interest on everything from the day you buy it, even if you pay on time.

Remedy: Throw the offer out!

Disappearing Benefits. Many banks enticed you to sign up with extra benefits such as lifetime warranty, a 5% discount on all travel, or protection if an item purchased is lost. Some banks have now cut back on these extras without the fanfare that launched them.

Remedy: Read annual disclosure of changes, and switch cards if need be.

Double Fees On Cash Advances. Most credit cards impose both finance charges and a transaction fee on cash advances. Interest starts from the day of the advance, and the transaction fee can be up to 2.5% of the amount taken. Beware of cards advertising "no finance charges." Transaction fees may still apply.

Remedy: Limit cash advances.

Misleading Monthly Minimums. You may think it is beneficial to have a card where you only need to pay 2%-3% of your balance monthly. It is just the opposite. The bank stands to make far more money from finance charges the longer you carry out payments—and you foot the bill.

Remedy: Pay all you can monthly.

Do You Need a Credit Card?

Most of us only *need* a credit card for booking flights, hotels, renting cars, and buying online. But, for the sake of convenience (or because we don't have the money for our purchases), we use credit cards so frequently that we are fast approaching a cashless society. If we could manage credit card spending effectively, there wouldn't be a problem.

Whenever we pull out that little piece of plastic, we buy our tomorrow with money we don't have today. The process is fast and convenient and it often gives us a buzz of excitement.

GP: "I have a trick for managing credit card spending; I wrote this on a piece of paper and keep folded around my credit card:

Is this a **NEED** or a **WANT**?

It makes me think twice when I'm tempted to buy something I haven't planned for."

Your Personal Money Vault

Credit and debit cards can be a convenient method to manage purchases, provided your financial life is in your control. Until it is, use these three techniques to discipline your indiscriminate use of plastic money:

1. The Vault Technique: Place each of your credit cards in a separate, water-filled container and place them in the freezer. Each time you are tempted to use a credit card, you'll have to thaw it out from its frozen vault. By the time you retrieve the card, you'll be clear on whether your spending is necessary or just an unplanned want.

2. Start living mostly on cash. The inconvenience of withdrawing cash before you buy anything will help you discipline your money habits. Only take enough money with you to get through the day.

3. Debit cards can be almost as dangerous to an undisciplined money-manager. Create awareness by wrapping your debit card with a piece of paper that questions why you are about to use it.

The Solution to Debt

Don't settle for being a willing victim; use GP's techniques to get out of debt and STAY out of debt. Getting rid of your debt is simple, but you WILL have to change some of your behaviours, which isn't always easy, especially at first. But I can tell you from experience that ANYONE can get out of debt by using the simple, practical techniques in the following pages.

Once out of debt, you'll find that the pleasure of not creating debt far exceeds the momentary thrill of buying something on credit that you don't really need, can't afford, and won't really care about all that much once you get it home.

Pay Off High-Interest Debt

The best investment most borrowers can make is to pay off consumer debt with double-digit interest rates. For example, if you have a $5,000 credit card balance at 19.8%, and are making the minimum payments, you will pay over $950 in interest the first year, $900+ in the second year, and so forth. You can see why lenders like giving you credit cards—you'll be providing them with huge profits for a long time to come.

Five-Step Debt Resolution Plan

The following Five-Step Debt Resolution Plan will help you resolve financial issues, as well as help you integrate successful money management habits. You will note that this approach allows you to live a normal life while eliminating unnecessary debt.

How do you get out of debt and use that money towards other necessities, savings, and investments?

1: Keep only one or two cards and make them harder to use. There is no need to have more than one card, so pick the one with the lowest interest rate and cut up the rest. The one you keep should be an "emergency card." Use the Vault Technique or tape over the numbers and expiry date with a piece of tape on which is written, "Is this an emergency?"

2: Move your debt. If you have more than one credit card payment, consider moving debt from a card with a higher interest rate to one with a lower interest rate. This will lower the amount of money you are spending towards the interest and get you out of debt faster. A small decrease in the interest rate can make a big difference on the interest owed. Call your credit card company and ask what lower rates are available—give them the chance to match an offer another company has made to you if you transfer your balance.

3: Use the *Snowball Principle*. List all of your credit card debts and the amount you are paying each month. Pay off the lowest amount first. Then use that money to start paying off the second lowest amount, then the next, and the next.

Let's look at an example:

If you have a $7000, $5000, and $2000 card with payments of $150, $125, and $100, you will finish paying off the $2000 card first. Once it is paid off, you take that $100 and put it towards the $5000 credit card. That means you are now paying $225/month. You have increased your payments which will pay off that credit card sooner and will have you paying a lot less in interest. Once that is paid off, you apply the $225 to the $7000 card, making your monthly payment $375. This will greatly accelerate the payment of this card, reducing your interest payments even further. When everything is paid off, you now have $375 extra each month to put towards savings or investments!

The Snowball Principle
1. Using the following table, fill in your debt repayment schedule.
2. Ensure that the rate of interest is correct.
3. In the last row, prioritize your repayment (do you want to pay the debt with the smallest amount owing? With the highest interest rate? The one that is the most important to your lifestyle?).

Lender	Amount Owing	Minimum Payment	Months to Pay Off# of payments *remaining*	Interest rate	Amount OwingAdditional amount *monthly*	Prioritize
Bay Card	$700	$30 + $75 = $105	Jan – Sep 2009	28%	$700	1
Visa	$2000	$25 + $$105 = $130	Sep 09 – Mar 2011	17%	$2000	2
Student Loan	$6000	$300 +$130 = $430	April 2011 –July 2012	8%	$6000	3

You can see that in the example above, the "snowball" began by the debtor applying an extra $75 a month to the Bay Card, which was then paid off in 9 months and, as each debt is eliminated and the payment rolled into the next one, payments proceed faster, so that the student loan of $6,000 is paid off a mere 15 months after it benefits from the "snowball."

4: **Renegotiate the terms of your loans with your creditors.** In some rare cases, your creditors may be willing to change the terms of your loans. More often, it will take the intervention of a professional debt counselor before an institution will give you better terms.

5: **Get help.** This seems obvious, but most people are unsure what to do during a debt crisis. A professional debt counselor can show you strategies for debt elimination and negotiate with creditors on your behalf.

By diligently employing these debt elimination tools, you can be free of debt slavery within two to seven years, depending on the extent of your debt-load.

When it comes to the "Buy it now" messages, remember that today's new toy won't be new tomorrow.

NUTS AND BOLTS

Debt Formula
Take Control & Repay Debt
Become master of your credit, rather than its slave. Now is the time to take control of your debt and credit cards. Find out where that money goes and put a stop to the leakage.

D—iscipline of actions
E—xcellence of attitude
B—udget all your resources
T—ime to repay your debt

Make a commitment to regain control of your life.

A LITTLE INSPIRATION

THE DREAM BOAT

After a wonderful day on the lake on a friend's boat, Suzie and Ron, both practicing lawyers decided that they wanted to own a boat, too. On a whim, they went to a boat show and impulsively came home with a brand new boat. It didn't seem too bad—with a little scrimping here and there and by stretching their credit cards they could pull it off!

Then they realized that they would need a bigger vehicle to tow their boat to the water. Plus there were marina fees. Since Jane's car was getting old they decided to buy an SUV. Soon, the additional monthly carrying costs of their two new purchases meant that they both had to work longer hours and had less time to enjoy their boat and SUV. With all the extra work, they went boating exactly three times that first summer!

The next spring a friend told them about a cottage on a beautiful lake only half an hour's drive away. If they sold the boat, stopped paying marina and insurance fees, and sold their SUV they could afford both a more gas friendly car for Jane and a mortgage on the cottage. They took the plunge and purchased the cottage. Now they can spend a lot less time working and much more time enjoying each other's company at the lake.

Chapter 5

BIG TICKET ITEMS
WHAT THEY REALLY COST

*"If we could sell our experiences for
what they cost us we'd be millionaires."*
Abigail Van Buren

> *"Owning a home is a keystone of wealth; both financial affluence and emotional security."* ~ Suze Orman

GP: "Here's one of the big lies: car payments are a way of life and you will always have one. Most people who finance a car purchase will buy a brand new one when they trade their car in after paying off the old one (if they actually keep the car long enough to pay it off). This belief traps them in car payments all through life."

Do You Really Need that Car?

Did you know:

- You can still enjoy a tax write-off through straight-line depreciation (as assets like cars and computers age they lose value)?
- The average monthly new car payment is $445 on a car valued at $25,550? *(Stats Canada 2006 Report #11-621-MIE)*

Let's Play!

GP: "Charles, I know you want to buy your first car. If you don't mind waiting, you can buy a brand new car in seven years. And you'll be earning interest, instead of paying it! But that's a little too long of a wait, so let's see how we can make this work.

Start by using that $4,000 you saved up from working in the garage on weekends for the last couple of years. You can get an older car in good running condition without owing a cent.

Now, if you had borrowed the money to purchase your car, you would need to repay the lender, right? Then make this payment to yourself in a separate savings account for your next car right away. Put $350 away every month. In two years, you'll have $8,400 plus a little bit of interest earned to buy your next car with. This time you can get a newer car, maybe one that's only three years old with low mileage and a year left to run on a lease. At the end of a year, you now own the car outright.

Keep on putting that $350 in the bank and in four years you'll have $16,800 plus interest. You can probably sell your old car for $3000, so now you have $20,000 to buy a brand new car.

- You can drive it for five years and sell it when you are ready for a new car. But just keep putting that $350 a month in the bank and you'll never have to pay a lick of interest or worry about the bank taking your car away. Of course, you can do even better if you are willing to buy last year's model! "

> The average Canadian lease for a new car is $24,000 over a 4 year period with a monthly payment of $418. At the end of that time, the car is worth less than $3,000. And then most people wonder—Who Took My Money?

Buy a Home & be Mortgage Free before you Retire

GP: "Charles, since buying a home will probably be your largest expense, finding ways to pay off the mortgage quickly would be wise The strategy I used and showed my kids was to convert the basement into a rental apartment. Instead of collecting junk in the basement, you make a portion of your home profitable for you.

Let me give you the definition of the word mortgage—The term comes from Old French and means 'dead pledge'."

Charles: "Does that mean that I shouldn't buy a home?"

GP: "No, a home is a great asset and we all need a place to live. But buy your home with your head as well as your heart and care for it afterwards so that it becomes part of your financial well-being instead of your financial stress!"

The largest asset of most people is the family home. Once the last mortgage payment is made, their housing expenses drop dramatically. They also have an asset that can be borrowed on in emergencies or converted into cash if they decide to sell it.

One of the highest financial priorities of Canadian homeowners is to pay off their mortgage as quickly as possible. Most are aware that paying down extra principal in the early years by whatever means possible can shorten the life of a mortgage and dramatically lower the interest paid over the long haul. The following "Pay-Off Tips" describe some of the most effective methods to achieve this goal.

Be Mortgage Free Faster

- **Increase your mortgage payment to highest that you can afford.** Most lenders will let you bring it down again if you were a little too enthusiastic in calculating how much you could pay or if your situation changes.

- **Use your RRSP refund to put into your mortgage.** Even if you borrowed (at prime) to buy your RRSP and use the tax refund to pay down your mortgage, you still come out ahead.

- **Bi-weekly payments.** This will painlessly reduce the principal owed by one full monthly payment each year.

- **Use double-up privileges.** Most mortgage agreement allows for double-up payments, so take advantage of it.

- **Round your payments up.** Even a small increase (e.g., rounding up from $1,245 to $1,260) will save substantial interest and the small sums are painless to part with.

- **Pay a lump sum whenever possible.** Decreasing the principal owed on your mortgage means that you pay less interest, which speeds up the process of becoming mortgage free.

- **Keep payments the same.** When you negotiate a lower rate, keep paying the same amount as with your old mortgage agreement—you will pay down more principal, pay less interest, and be mortgage free sooner.

- **Make bigger mortgage payments.** As your income gets bigger, rather than spending all of your raise on impulse purchases, increase the amount of your mortgage payments.

NUTS AND BOLTS

It ALWAYS pays to put down as much cash as possible when buying items that depreciate in value over time (the average car loses about 30% of its value in only one year—so if you buy last year's model, you let someone else eat up the depreciation). The shorter your payment schedule, the more money you take out of the item when you decide to sell it.

DON'T WASTE YOUR HARD-EARNED MONEY ON INTEREST!

Remember: What you don't have to pay in interest could go towards purchase of WANTS— the fun stuff!

A LITTLE INSPIRATION

WINDOW SHOPPING

In the clothing industry a suit that costs less than $30 to make can sell for a $1000 if it has the right designer label. Why? Because the person buying it believes the advertiser's claims that this suit is better than one with the same fabric and design but a less prestigious label.

Chapter 6

MONEY & RELATIONSHIPS

*"Rich people start off as poor people. The difference
is they take the nickels and dimes and they invest it
— they didn't spend it all at the mall."*
Ric Edelman

"The only reason a great many... families don't own an elephant is that they have never been offered an elephant for a dollar down and easy weekly payments." ~ Mad Magazine

- Are your money values lined up with your core values?
- Do you walk the walk, or just talk the talk?

GP: "Your relationship with money is essential to a good family core. It's not stressful when it's done right. Your relationship with your money is where it starts and spreads to the rest of the family. When you get married, you each bring different backgrounds and values. You need to find a way to meet without it tearing you apart. Learn to accommodate each other. I believe it is important to include your kids in the money decision process, so that you teach them healthy money habits."

Discovering Passion & Fun

Compromises are a process of both parties giving up what they think they want, in order to find something they both want more. Understand where both your viewpoints come from and find a way to meet each other's needs and wants.

Relationship with Money

With money as a daily partner, it is wise to keep clear guidelines and expectations when dealing with it. Money should not consume much of your time, as it can cloud reality and confound happiness, taking focus off the important aspects of life like your partner and family.

Wisdom tells us "seek your bliss" and "follow your passion" and as inevitable as the sunrise, the money magically follows. This has proven true in my life countless times as the cycles repeat themselves.

Defining Values & Life Purpose

Most people today grow up in families that never discuss money; consequently, they never learn the importance of the workings of everyday finances. The silence in these cases is literally deafening!

This silence teaches children to avoid being open with loved ones about issues involving money, not to mention that their parents never model money-conflict resolution skills.

Satisfaction

When are you satisfied? It is different for everyone. You first have to understand and know what will satisfy YOU. If you need a mansion and a race car to feel satisfied, your time commitment to wealth is going to be different than if your satisfaction lies in a simple family cottage, a car in good working order, tuition for your children, and so forth.

Success has a Price

If you are not careful, the time commitment, the habits you need to change, and the energy that will go into creating wealth can take you away from your family and friends. If you do it alone, you are almost guaranteed to be lonely when you reach your goal. Instead, do it together with your family and you will be successful on many levels. After all, does success mean being extremely wealthy, or does it mean being stress free and living manageably?

NUTS AND BOLTS

Life is beautiful and you need to live every moment of it to the fullest—but that's very hard to do if you are worried about money or living in debt slavery. If you have "problematic" indebtedness, it completely overtakes your life. The cycle of worry, deprivation, and harmful "feel-good" splurges overwhelm any chance of happiness or even just plain relaxation.

A LITTLE INSPIRATION

THE HEART OF THE ROSE

Tibetan monks use this ancient technique to focus their thoughts and shed negative emotions. You can use a rose, a pine cone or a traditional Mandela. Just choose something that you find beautiful and care to contemplate.

Each morning, go to the garden and pick a fresh rose. Then sit in your favorite quiet spot and, holding the rose in the center of your hand, stare at it. Focus on the wonderful colour; look at the heart of the rose. At first you will become distracted, but this is because your concentration "muscle" has not been exercised.

Do not let any negative thoughts enter your mind; just think of the rose and its beauty. This will show you how to concentrate and force you to store ONLY positive thoughts. Every time during the day that a negative thought crosses your mind, just think of the Heart of the Rose. It may sound silly to you now, but you will see that this method calms you and clears your mind. In just a few weeks, you will notice that you are able to focus exclusively on the positive. In order to succeed you MUST do this exercise every morning for 5 minutes before beginning your day.

Any and all forms of meditation clear the mind of distractions and allow all these pieces of information to combine into thousands and thousands of different patterns. The mind loves to work on puzzles and problems. "There are no problems, only opportunities." Whether it's a positive thought or the solution to a problem, give your mind the opportunity to be your friend. Use a prayer, a mantra, or a focused thought to listen to "the voice within."

Chapter 7

MIND OVER MONEY

"Money is neither my god nor my devil. It is a form of energy that tends to make us more of who we already are, whether it's greedy or loving."

Dan Millman

"You are today where your thoughts have brought you; you will be tomorrow where your thoughts take you." ~ James Allen

GP: "Charles, your mind is like the motor of your car; just as the oil you put in has to be the very best, you should choose to insert only good and positive thoughts into your mind. The brain doesn't differentiate between right and wrong or good and bad; It takes all information in. You have to train it to judge and eliminate the "bad" messages; the ones that will hurt you in the long run."

You must maintain responsibility for your relationship with money. Money does not bring happiness. Rather, it is how you feel about yourself that determines contentment.

- Do you value peace of mind?
- What impact does financial freedom have on your happiness?

Core Beliefs About Money

Each day is a new experience and opportunity. You possess the power to chase out negative beliefs from the past and replace them with positive ones. PRACTICE!

Negative Belief	Positive Belief
I was born to fail.	Hard work and determination can make dreams come true.
The system favors the rich.	The system favours those who live within their means and, resultantly, pay bills on time. These people are not rich; they combine good judgment and discipline.
You can't trust anybody.	Many caring people help others. It is their nature and they know it fulfills them.
Money doesn't grow on trees.	It's not how much you make. It's what you do with what you make that counts.
I'm not going to drive someone else's old car!	Buying a new car is the worst possible decision, due to the immediate depreciation and years of high monthly payments.

Negative Belief	Positive Belief
My car, my house, and my toys equal my success.	The happiness of living without worry and experiencing inner peace is the ultimate success. Our lives are meant to have a deeper meaning; we weren't put on this earth to have more "stuff" than the next guy.
Rich people are dishonest.	While we've all witnessed examples of bad behaviour by people with too much money, there is a human tendency to paint all wealthy people with the same brush.

Money permits you to experience life to its fullest, but unless you reach an inner peace, you will find that life still presents the same challenges despite a higher income.

Many people with high incomes aren't satisfied with their financial reality and believe "more" will make them happy. These people never have enough and they are condemned to the treadmill of financial unhappiness until they learn to question their current values and money habits and to be happy with what they have.

Money can be a tool for personal development. Whether you believe you have too little or too much, you are absolutely right!

Exploring Core Beliefs
Thoughts

The quality of your thoughts determines the quality of your life. If you think that something you want is possible, then you will take the time to figure out what steps and actions you need to take to make your dream real. But when you think that something is impossible, it is!

- Thoughts are small little packages of energy; vital and alive.
- Thoughts are the beginning of creation.
- Thoughts lead to action when emotionally connected (positively or negatively).

Faith

When you have faith, you move gracefully through any difficult period in your life. Faith gives the strength to make the changes that give financial freedom. With faith in your heart, you'll trust that the age of your car doesn't matter to the girl you want to ask out.

- Faith gives a purpose to life.
- True faith can heal doubt and anxiety and permit us to obtain inner peace and happiness.

Emotions

You will never know your own greatness until you learn to deal with your feelings/emotions and learn why you react the way you do. Are you in control of your money emotions or do you let your emotions control what you do? When a negative emotion surfaces, how will you deal with it?

Everything in your life is controlled by the way you deal with your emotions and what you choose to store in your brain as "true and good." Learn to deal with your emotions and your money by *planning* in *advance.* Everything is possible!

Fear

Fear is like a flat tire that immobilizes you until you can repair it. It takes away your ability to move forward and your hope for the future. Fear is the enemy of creativeness and optimism.

Fear is a poor motivator over the course of a life time. You know that falling off a cliff is going to hurt, but in your everyday life you aren't obsessed with the idea that you'll walk off a cliff. If your money controls you, then you are always in danger of walking blindly over a financial precipice.

A lot of your energy, time, and emotions go into worrying. When *you* own your money, then you are free from fear and can put time, passion, and, yes, your money, into making your dreams a solid reality.

Attitude

Genius is 1% inspiration and 99% perspiration.

- You can achieve major lifetime dreams and goals sooner with the right attitude.
- You can earn more money and become financially free.

- You can create a new truth about money to silence your fear.

Attitude has more value than our past experiences, failures, or successes. Each of us has the power to choose what attitude we will exhibit each and every day. We do not have the power to change the past or the actions of others, but we are the master of our attitude.

Choose to see life with a joyful attitude.

Passion

Without passion, you will never achieve financial manageability, a happy relationship, or a career you enjoy. Nothing is changed until you believe in yourself enough to transform your passion into action. To reach maximum productivity, your body, heart, and mind must all enthusiastically say "Yes!"

Anything that you do with passion is yours; it can't be taken away.

NUTS AND BOLTS

As children, we are often taught that money is dirty, that there isn't enough money, that rich people are greedy. These early teachings influence our later approach to finances, often with disastrous results.

Usually, when one has financial problems, the true reasons have nothing to do with money.

You MUST train your brain to recognize negative and self-destructive thoughts and concentrate on the positive so that each day represents a new opportunity to make your life better. PRACTICE!

A LITTLE INSPIRATION

LEAPING THE CHASM

There was a man whose unhealthy and harmful behaviors put him in hospital. He decided to find a mentor to guide him through the process of healing him of those habits. His mentor stated clearly that this journey to health would require great change and extraordinary commitment.

Within a few weeks of beginning his life-changing path, he repeated the same behavior and found himself back in the hospital. His mentor paid him a visit and said, "You accepted me as your mentor and committed yourself to follow my guidance without question. But here you are in hospital again, almost dead. I cannot continue as your mentor because you have failed to honor your word to me. Until you understand that no one can leap a chasm in two jumps, you will never understand the power of commitment."

Chapter 8

MASTERING MONEY HABITS

*"People only accept change when they are faced
with necessity, and only recognise necessity
when a crisis is upon them."*
Jean Monnet

"Insanity is repeating the same actions, over and over, again and again, and expecting different results." ~ Albert Einstein

GP: "Based on other attempts, people might think they don't have it in them to change how they deal with money. But that's probably because they set themselves up for failure in the past by making changes so drastic that only one person in a million could stick to them. Don't let this happen to you, son."

COMMITMENT

GP: "You know you are in danger the moment you begin to forget your commitment."

Pledge to yourself:
- I'm taking control of my life and nobody can stop me.
- I'm committing to be my best, all day long, every single day.
- I'm going to keep going when everyone else is ready to quit.
- I'm spending my time on activities that recharge instead of drain me.
- I am capable of getting as much work done in the last hour of the day as in the first one.
- I have the power to plow through obstacles and setbacks without undue strain (because I am going to look at this as a challenge that I am capable of mastering) and I will still have the energy to enjoy family, friends, and recreational activities.
- If I fall down one day, I will get up and dust myself off and start anew.

Ask Yourself:
What if I commit to do things differently today?
What if I commit to change to be free of debt and always keep enough money to meet my needs?

 YES! I make a promise to myself to change my habits so that I can achieve financial freedom.

Desire to Change
I AM READY TO TAKE CHARGE

My financial life begins when I am truly committed to taking charge of my money habits.

I know I am capable of making the changes required NOW in order to live a debt-free life.

I will examine my money habits honestly.

I will learn more about money in order to make better choices.

I will care for my money and make wise choices.

By making the decision to start right now, you have created the opportunity to expand your financial consciousness and change your life.

Changing Beliefs
Begin now by restating your beliefs:
- Change *money is hard to come by* to *money is abundant,* and open the door to opportunity.
- Change *money is evil, dirty, or bad* to *money is good and acceptable*, and create a healthy perspective about money.
- Change *money comes monthly* to *money comes from many directions*, and create doorways to opportunity
- Change *money is not for me* to *whom better than me for money to come to*, I deserve a good life (without worries) and I can then help others.
- Change *money is a man thing* to *I can understand and use money wisely*, I can learn this.
- Change *money is good medicine* to *money is a means to improve my life*, if I handle it properly.
- Change *money is a menace* to *money is a solution*.

The choice is yours and, since you are reading this book, you have already taken a huge step to realizing your limitless financial potential. By beginning right now, you create the opportunity to raise your financial consciousness and change your life forever.

NUTS AND BOLTS

Change old habits and beliefs that control your life. Prepare for a life without financial worries!

- Transform your PASSION into unbridled ACTION.
- Expect success rather than fear failure.
- Focus on solutions rather than remaining stuck in the problem.
- Speak and act with more enthusiasm.
- Enjoy life with a positive attitude and a passion for a bright future.

Focus is essential to success in any endeavor.

Remember: You are beginning a whole new aspect of your life. It will take time and practice until you master these lessons.

THE TWO WOLVES

Sitting by the fire, an ancient Cherokee warrior was asked by his grandson about the fiercest battle he had ever fought.

"My child," he replied, "the greatest battle I know is between two wolves. These wolves live in each human being. One is Evil. It is anger, envy, resentment, self-pity, lust, lies, false pride, greed, arrogance, festering sorrow, and ego. The other is Good. It is love, peace, joy, serenity, kindness, humility, generosity, compassion, faith, and truth."

After a moment, the grandson asked, "Which wolf will win?"

"That is simple," replied the old warrior, "The one you feed the most."

How do the "Evil" wolf's traits affect your pocket? How about false pride? Have you ever gone out to a dinner or bought a gift that was beyond your means because you didn't want a friend in a higher salary bracket to know that money was tight? How about feeling justified in going on a spending binge when you are angry with your spouse? Have you lied to yourself that you have the money to buy something when you know that you don't?

On the other hand, when the "Good" wolf is fed, you don't need to spend money boosting your self-esteem by pretending to be at a standard of living that is beyond your means. You'll have more fun treating your wealthier friends to home-cooked bowls of spaghetti and a night of cards and laughter than you would at a fancy restaurant that you can't afford—and they'll respect you for it.

Chapter 9

NEEDS, WANTS & DESIRES – GET CLEAR!

*"You can never get enough of what
you don't need to make you happy."*
Eric Hoffer

> *"You have succeeded in life when all you really want*
> *is only what you really need." ~* Vernon Howard

GP: "You want a new sound system for your room, but, on the other hand, you need to replace the worn tires on your car."

Do You Need it—or Want it?

One of the keys to taking control of your money is in knowing the difference between needs, wants, and desires. That can be tough, as marketers spend a fortune convincing us that they are one and the same. But if you stop and think for a minute, your inner voice tells you the truth. Use reason to challenge the impulse to buy.

Needs are necessary for our comfort and our survival. They include food, shelter, and SOME clothing.

Wants are emotional urges that can override wisdom. Think of high-end electronics, constant home remodeling, Jimmy Choo shoes, etc.

GP: "Here's one way I figure out my wants: if I earn $22 per hour and want to buy something for $22, I am spending an hour of my life. I quantify all potential purchases with two questions:
- How many hours do I have to work to pay for it?
- Is it worth the time out of my life? "

Desires are deeper, long term yearnings that come from deep within. They include the desire for romantic love, family, education, and meaningful work.

When your *wants* control you, your spending is pretty much guaranteed to be out of control.

GP: "Think about things that you want and write them out in the same way as you see on the following chart. This will reinforce your understanding and practice of intuition, an invaluable tool in achieving your goals."

Let's Play!

Needs Necessities of Life		Wants Based on Emotion
	Leather coat	X
X	New suit for work	
	Designer jeans	X
X	Snow tires	
	Sports car	X
X	Replace work shoes	
X	Winter coat	
	Scented pillar candle	X
	Plasma TV	X

Making changes in your financial approach doesn't mean that you cannot fulfill your wants. It just means you will have to take care of your needs first. When you stick to this approach, you will eventually own a mortgage-free home, have savings for family needs, pay off your credit cards before the interest comes due, AND you will have even more money for your wants.

Are you thinking, "Hey, where's the FUN in that?" The fun comes because you can now enjoy spending money on your wants without the stress that comes from putting your needs on the backburner. In fact, paying for your wants will be more fun because you will have much more money than you have now. It may take a bit longer, but it will be stress free and yours to enjoy.

NUTS AND BOLTS

Before you spend money, ask yourself the following questions:
- Do I need it, or just want it?
- What other costs are involved?
- What will spending this money do to my lifestyle?
- Am I buying this to meet an emotional need or to compensate for something else?

Avoid Temptation
- Don't go shopping when you feel emotional.
- Never buy groceries when you are hungry.
- Don't go into that expensive store with things that you know you can't afford (why torture yourself).

What you don't see won't tempt you to make a foolish purchase that you don't need and that you'll regret later. Just imagine how this could change your life.

Plan AHEAD.
Identify your needs and wants and write them down.

A LITTLE INSPIRATION

THE CATERPILLAR CIRCLE

The famous French naturalist Jean-Henri Fabre observed the curious phenomena of caterpillar circles. He put a group of them on the rim of a large flowerpot and the caterpillars all connected to each other in a complete circle as they kept crawling slowly around and around the pot. The scientist thought that they would split up and make their way down the side of the pot towards food.

There was plenty of food a few feet away. But the caterpillars never broke their circle. Instead, ignoring the nearby food, they walked around and around the pot for several days until they were too weak to continue.

Luckily, we aren't caterpillars. Even if you are currently using much of your energy to go round and round in unproductive and unfulfilling activities (and your financial life mirrors this), you can break away from the cycle at any time you choose to do so.

Chapter 10

REINVENTING FINANCES

"The reinvention of daily life means marching off the edge of our maps."

Bob Black

"The art of living easily, as to money, is to pitch your scale of living one degree below your means." ~ Sir Henry Taylor

GP: "Charles, just as it is important to always keep the garage clean and put away our tools when we finish working at night, knowing where to find important documents is a must."

Charles: "I know GP, this is on my 'to do' list, but I never seem to find the time to get to it. I work almost every evening in the garage and weekends, well, weekends are for fun. So the papers end up getting shoved in the bottom drawer of my dresser."

Get Your House in Order

Let's Play

Get an accordion file and keep it near to wherever you empty your pockets and put your mail. You can create a very simple tag system inside the accordion file. A few files are all you need to place your important documents in order. Then just take two minutes every night and put your receipts and bills inside. It will make your life a lot easier and save you hours of time.

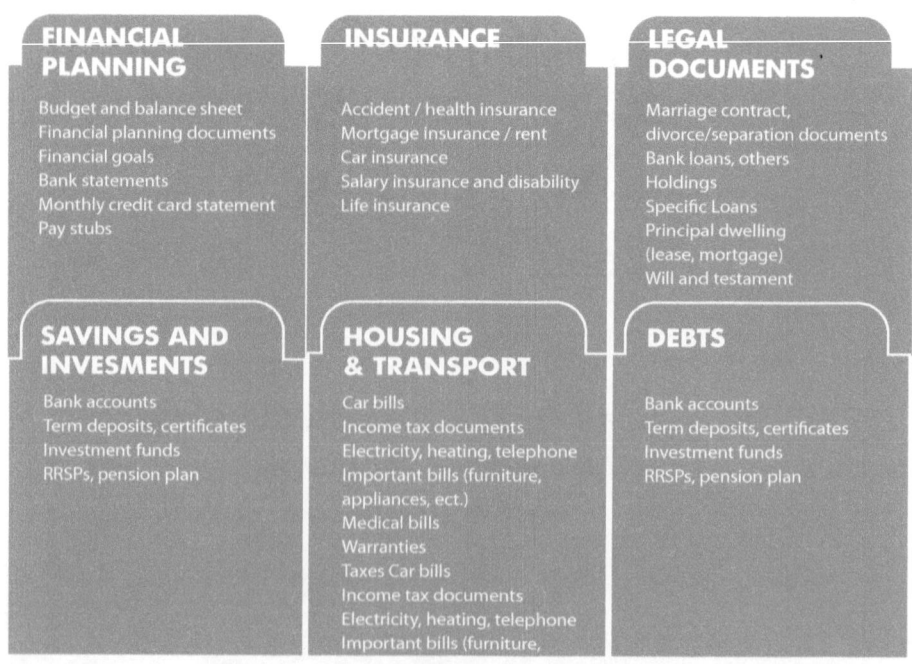

FINANCIAL PLANNING
Budget and balance sheet
Financial planning documents
Financial goals
Bank statements
Monthly credit card statement
Pay stubs

INSURANCE
Accident / health insurance
Mortgage insurance / rent
Car insurance
Salary insurance and disability
Life insurance

LEGAL DOCUMENTS
Marriage contract,
divorce/separation documents
Bank loans, others
Holdings
Specific Loans
Principal dwelling
(lease, mortgage)
Will and testament

SAVINGS AND INVESMENTS
Bank accounts
Term deposits, certificates
Investment funds
RRSPs, pension plan

HOUSING & TRANSPORT
Car bills
Income tax documents
Electricity, heating, telephone
Important bills (furniture,
appliances, ect.)
Medical bills
Warranties
Taxes Car bills
Income tax documents
Electricity, heating, telephone
Important bills (furniture,

DEBTS
Bank accounts
Term deposits, certificates
Investment funds
RRSPs, pension plan

1. FINANCIAL PLANNING
- Budget and balance sheet
- Financial planning documents
- Financial goals
- Bank statements
- Monthly credit card statement
- Pay stubs

2. INSURANCE
- Accident / health insurance
- Mortgage insurance / rent
- Car insurance
- Salary insurance and disability
- Life insurance

3. LEGAL DOCUMENTS
- Marriage contract, divorce/separation documents
- Bank loans, others
- Holdings
- Specific Loans
- Principal dwelling (lease, mortgage)
- Will and testament

4. SAVINGS AND INVESMENTS
- Bank accounts
- Term deposits, certificates
- Investment funds
- RRSPs, pension plan

5. HOUSING & TRANSPORT
- Car bills
- Income tax documents
- Electricity, heating, telephone
- Important bills (furniture, appliances, ect.)
- Medical bills
- Warranties
- Taxes

6. DEBTS
- Personal loan
- Credit Cards

GP: Now that we are in the paper stuff let's look at an important paper that is the concern of man consumers.

"Charles, the credit report score is starting to be a big concern in many people's life. It shouldn't be, simply because when you pay bills on time, even just the minimum due (more is always better), you'll have no problem.

Your credit report is used by lenders to evaluate loan risks. If you have a good history of payments, many companies will be willing to lend you money. Utility companies also use credit scores to determine the size of the deposit they will ask for before connecting services such as phone, gas, cable, internet, hydro, etc."

Your Credit Report & Why it Matters

The most commonly used scoring method, the Beacon Score, ranges from 300 to 900. As long as you have a score of 700 or higher, you can expect better interest rates, especially on larger loans like a mortgage.

The 5 factors that affect your Credit Score:

Payment History	35%
Current Debts	30%
Age of Accounts	15%
Type of Credit	10%
Credit Enquiries	10%

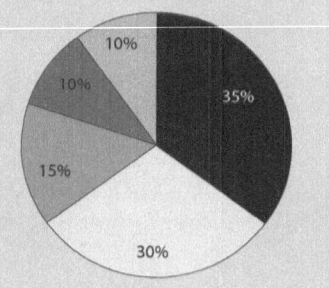

Respect Your Word

The single biggest factor that impacts your credit score is whether you pay your bills on time. Pay your credit card and loans on time and you will have good credit.

The next factor is your current debt. If your credit card balances are over 75% of their limit, your score goes down considerably. If you can bring your cards down below 50% of their outstanding balance, your score will go up very quickly.

The stability in your credit is also a factor you need to consider. The older the credit history, showing good standing, stability, and repayment, the better your credit will be.

If you know that you are going to be looking to buy a house in the near future, stop making credit applications. Too many inquiries in a short peroid of time tend to scare lenders.

With a little thought and awareness, you have the power to improve your credit scores. If you manage your credit effectively, you won't have to worry about your credit report; it will be in good standing.

Your Credit Score is Free to Request

Your credit score information is free when you order it from the credit bureaus (see *page 145* for credit bureau contact information). It takes a little longer to get it by mail, but it is free. If you can't wait, you can buy it online.

Alert

Anyone who calls themselves a credit "clean up" guru is cheating you out of much needed money. You are the clean up guru for your personal finances. Pay your bills on time and you'll never need to ask what your credit score is.

GP: "Ok Charles, now let's do a little exercise that will need to be done once and then revisited each year; your net worth. This is the difference between all the things of value that you own and all the debts you owe."

The Snapshot – Your Net Worth Statement

A Net Worth Statement is a **snapshot** (picture) of your financial worth at a precise date. It will help in planning financial strategy for the future, and will give you important clues about where you should concentrate your financial planning efforts. Net Worth Statements are also useful for other purposes, such as when applying for a mortgage, credit card, car loan, or college financial aid for your kids.

GP: "Do you really know where you stand financially? In order to get control of your finances and plan your financial future effectively, you need to first know where you stand today."

Charles: "How do you do that? "

GP: "First let me explain these two important words, ASSETS and LIABILITIES."

- *Assets* are the value you hold in possessions, savings, stocks, etc. (they return money in your pocket).
- *Liabilities* are the debts you owe (they remove money from your pocket).

*Your net worth is your **assets** minus your **liabilities**.*

Calculating your net worth is fairly simple (*see Net Worth Worksheet on the included CD*).

First, list everything you can think of and total your assets (the things of value that you own):

- **Cash** and cash equivalents, such as Certificates of Deposit, money market accounts, bank accounts.
- **Investments**, such as stocks, bonds, mutual funds, savings bonds.
- **Retirement funds**, such as Retirement plans, company pension plans, including only the amounts you are fully vested in.
- **Real estate**, including your home and any other real estate or personal property such as boats, cars, RVs, and planes.
- **Household and personal goods**, such as furnishings, jewelry, furs, collectibles, antiques. Use the estimated fair market value (the price a rational buyer would pay). For cars, use the blue book value.

Second, list all amounts you owe and then total your liabilities:

- **Loans**, including your mortgage, student loans, bank loans, and car loans.
- **Credit card balances**, including major bank cards, store cards, and gas cards.

- **Taxes owed**, such as real estate taxes or income taxes.
- Any **miscellaneous** amounts that you owe.

  Now **subtract** your **liabilities** from your **assets**.

If the number is positive, then you have more assets than liabilities. You have a positive net worth. If so, give yourself a pat on the back and start planning on how to increase your net worth. If the number is negative (more liabilities than assets), don't despair; use the Tool Kit to get on the road to financial health.

Tip: For a general idea of what your net worth should be, multiply your annual income by your age and divide by ten. For example, if you are 46 years old and earn $50,000 a year, your net worth should be:

$$\$50,000 \times 46 \text{ years} \div 10 = \$230,000$$

Let's Play
My Financial Snapshot - **NET WORTH**

Assets		Liabilities	
House value	$300,000	Mortgage	$254,000
Vehicle	8,000	Car loan	3,700
RRSPs	10,000	Credit card debt	4,800
Chequing account	250		
Total assets	**$318,250**	**Total liabilities**	**$262,500**
		Net worth	**$55,750**

You should monitor your progress periodically to keep track of your net worth.

NUTS AND BOLTS

Being organized will save hours, leaving more time for fun and you will never worry about your credit score again.

Pay your loans on time
- Have no outstanding balance over your credit limit.
- Minimize revolving credit.

Know where you stand financially today
- Take the time to create your snapshot.

You need to have a clear picture of where you stand financially before you move on to your current expenses and how to manage them.

A LITTLE INSPIRATION

- There is a significant difference between goals and dreams.
- First we have a dream.
- Then we want to fulfill our dream.
- Just as it is unwise to start a drive from New York to Vancouver without preparing a roadmap, so it is with achieving dreams, visions, and purpose.

Chapter 11

FINANCIAL TOOL KIT

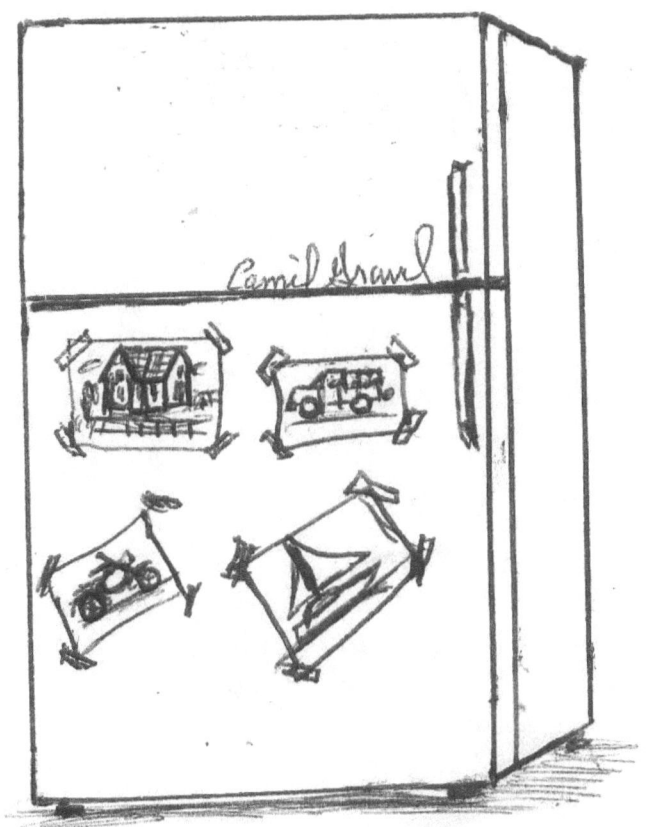

"Don't tell me where your priorities are. Show me where you spend your money and I'll tell you what they are."
James W. Frick

*"Tell me and I will forget. Show me and I will remember.
Let me do it and I will understand."* ~ Chinese Proverb

GP: "Charles, I know that budgeting is not much fun, but I will show you my method, the automatic/cash system. Just like when I taught you how to repair cars, the more you practice the easier it gets. Practice make perfect!

Remember one thing, the more you spend, the more time you need to spend earning it. It is a vicious cycle. A decision that seems like a great way to relax might even have the opposite effect if you do not plan effectively.

The whole point of learning how to manage money is to help make dreams come true. If you haven't become clear about your dreams, how can you achieve them?"

NEVER STOP DREAMING!
Believe you can and you will achieve your wildest dreams.

Achieving Your Dreams

As we go through life, we often get discouraged by the people who should support us—parents, teachers, friends, family, and co-workers. This is why many adults stop dreaming; they no longer believe in themselves enough to achieve their dreams.

GP: "We all have dreams, some grand, and some small. It doesn't matter how hard or how easy life is, we all have hopes for our future. For your dreams to come true, you must believe that someday, somehow, you will achieve them."

Why is it so important to live your dreams?

Because dreams give your life purpose, and knowing that your real dreams can come true will help you to remember why it is that you get up in the morning and head off to work.

All great fortunes started in someone's imagination. See yourself living in the home of your dreams, enjoying ideal relationships with friends and loved ones, contributing to the world through your own unique talents and abilities. Imagine the fortune you could create and the good it could do. Believe it and you will see it.

> *"Obstacles are those frightful things you see when you take your eyes off your goal."* ~ Henry Ford.

GP: "Goals are those planned, progressive steps that lead to the fulfillment of the dream. If you fail to plan, you've planned to fail."

GOAL SETTING = THE PLAN

The **PLAN** is what you would like to have accomplished or acquired at a specific time in your life. This is done by setting your goals. They provide you with focus, purpose, and direction for the way you live and determine the way you use money. They keep you motivated. Without goals, it is easy to get sidetracked and lose sight of your dreams.

The best way to set goals is to put them down in writing, as specifically and realistically as possible. Take time to research them, and ask yourself as many questions as possible to become clear about the specifics and you will achieve them sooner.

- Is this a short, intermediate, or long term goal?
- What do I need to do to achieve this dream?
- Do I cut back on other areas to be able to afford this goal?
- Can I think of another way to create the means to achieve it?
- Who has the ability to assist me in achieving it?
- When do I want to start and why?

Your subconscious mind holds all the rules, controls, and parameters for your life-experience. If you are to realize your goals they must match your present belief system. People who consistently realize their goals believe themselves worthy and capable of reaching them. Successful people thrive on challenges. They have conditioned their sub-conscious mind to "stretch," causing resistance to melt away. It's a journey, one that you can master with persistence.

It bears repeating: "Obstacles are what you'll see if you take your eye off the goal!"

If you set your goal to take a luxury cruise around the world and you expect to be enjoying shipboard life in less than a year when your annual income is less than $40,000, it's highly unlikely you'll reach your goal. On the other hand, if you set a goal for a cruise during the off season, with luxury at a price that you can afford, and you maintain your focus on that goal, it is possible.

Setting SMART Goals

When you set a goal, be **SMART** about it:

Specific – Be detailed, not vague

Measurable - To help you stay on track

Attainable - It must be possible

Realistic - It must be within reason

Timely - It must be set in a reasonable time frame

Write out your goals using the three Ws of what, why, and when.

What: What type of home? What price range?

Why: To stop giving my money to a landlord and have a place that I call home

When: Two years from now.

A general goal would be, "I want to buy a home."
*But a **SMART** goal would be:*

- I want a small bungalow home in a friendly neighborhood close to community facilities.
- I will set aside $500 per month for 24 months = $12,000 down payment.
- I will confine my house hunt to properties within my repayment capacities (30% of my income).
- The house will have an income suite.
- I will purchase my home two years from now, after saving 10% for my down payment.

Owning a home is now an attainable goal!

You reach your goal with a few simple changes. When you need inspiration to keep those changes going, review your dream list and reaffirm your commitment.

Let's Play!
How would you like to go on vacation each year without having to put in extra time working? There are many ways and endless options. Start having fun with numbers and see what you can come up with. The purpose is to show you how you can get **twice as much with the same money***.*

You want a swimming pool, a trip to the Caribbean, and you need a new roof.

My goals are MY DREAMS	Costs	# month	Savings	Project
Trip to the Caribbean	3,000	36	85.00	3
Swimming pool	2,000	24	85.00	2
Repair roof	1,500	12	125.00	1
Total costs	**6,500**			

Buy Now, Pay Later Attitude
You decide to borrow $6,500 at 12% interest on a 5 year period. This will cost you $295.00 a month for the next 5 years and you will have paid $2,175 in interest—almost enough for a whole *new* vacation.

This method keeps you chained to the cycle of debt slavery.

The Wise Choice
"Patience is a virtue," said the wise man. Plan carefully and you will have twice as much of what you really want. No one likes to pay interest. Instead, you could have more money for your wants.

Now start putting aside $300 per month in a separate account. In three months you will have $900; now you have the roof repaired (use your low rate credit card for the remaining $600 and pay $300 off before the grace period is up). By November the roof is all paid for and you pay interest on only $300.

Continue to set aside the $300 and, by next June, you will have $2,100—enough for the pool. The pool is installed in time to enjoy a fun summer and it is FULLY paid for.

Continue to set aside the same $300 and you will enjoy your trip to the Caribbean next March. You will have $2,700 in cash and you can place the remaining $300 on your credit card and pay it off before the grace period is over.

This method will cost you less than $50 in interest and you will enjoy everything that you want stress free.

When you are focused and have SMART goals in mind, you will discover that you get out of your own way and make the necessary changes to reach your goals.

By making a chart on paper, it is easier to prioritize, to visualize the challenges, and to figure out the plan. (*Use the CD's Goal Setting worksheet.*)

NUTS AND BOLTS

Success lies in knowledge and putting in the necessary effort. One cannot work without the other.
A Magic Formula for achieving your goals:

M + E2 = R

Method + Double Effort = Results
• Write down your dreams
• Visualize your dream (imagine it as a movie, feel the emotions)
• Allow enough time to achieve your dream
• Set goals. They must be **SMART**
(Specific / Measurable / Attainable / Realistic / Timely)

Most people take months to plan a trip. How many of us take the time to plan for the future?

GP: "Charles, how do you eat an elephant? A bite at a time! I'm teaching you the knowledge and techniques of proper money-management, but it is up to you to do the work. If you put these ideas to work, I guarantee you won't experience money stress, no matter how big or small your income is. Remember, knowing a technique doesn't mean much if you don't use it."

Charles: "GP is it true that more than 85% of the working population does not plan or track their expenses.

GP: "The most common excuse given is that they've tried budgeting and it doesn't work. Well, I agree."

The typical "starvation" budget layout doesn't work for most. It's like going on a strict weight-loss diet. Eventually, you just can't take the deprivation and you go right back to your old habits. Making a budget is not much fun, but you **must be a good manager of your money** in order to have the financial freedom to do whatever you want.

Don't Get Lost: MAP It

Mapping is the most recent term for that scary word "budgeting." There is no need for fear. A budget is simply a money map that lays out how you will use your financial resources, based on your expected earnings. Mapping is a method of keeping track of where your money goes. An impossibly strict budget is a bad one, as it sets you up for failure. You have to feel good about the choices you make and actions you take—and not constantly deprived of all pleasure.

I suggest that you create a 12 month map (budget). During this span, all expenses and income will usually occur at least once. Include your short, medium, and long term goals, so that you can track your progress through regular reviews.

Map out exactly how you are going to be spending every dollar that you earn so that it works for you. It's all about organizing your monthly expenses based on your income. This will help you to achieve your goals and fulfill your everyday needs and financial responsibilities, based on your actual circumstances. Follow your map as closely as possible. Why is this so important? Because *managed money works harder for you*.

This method puts YOU in control. Start by allocating your money with your existing obligations. Then ask yourself how you would like to allocate the remainder of your money and then spend accordingly. Create your own MAP, based on the sample below. Keep in mind that the total must always equal 100%.

Spouse #1	Income: $3,040
Spouse #2	Income: $2,375
Total Income: $5,415	

Expense Category Guideline

Savings / Investment
Housing **35–40%**
Food **5–15%**
Transport **8–10%**
Clothing **4–7%**
Education / Medical **5%**
Insurance **5%**
Personal / Debts or Recreational Activities **7-10%**

Expenses

10% - pay yourself first	**$550**		
Mortgage	2,020	Auto insurance	200
Car loan	300	Auto fuel	200
Pay down credit card debt	240	Auto maintenance	80
House insurance	70	Clothing & accessories	100
Property tax	120	Entertainment	100
Telephone	40	Medical/dental/vision care	100
Cablevision	40	Savings for new car	150
Utilities - heat, light	120	Dining out	145
Household furnishings	150	Internet access	40
Home maintenance	150	Life insurance	100
Groceries	400		
Total monthly expenses $5,415			

Once you know where your money is going you can allocate a certain amount of money to each expense category. If your expenses are more than you make, you'll need to adjust your allocations or eliminate certain expenses.

Paycheck Planner
An Automatic Habit that brings Financial Health

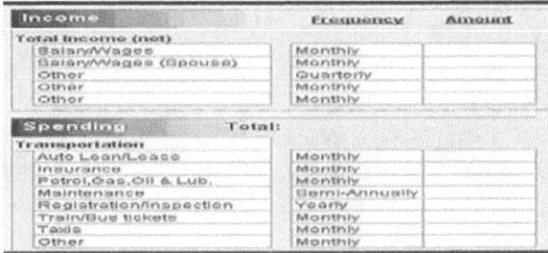

Your paycheck planner can be as simple as a little book where you put down how much each check you receive is worth, what you want to do with it each week, and if your assigned uses match up with your goals. It should include needs, fixed and variable expenses, and savings of both the long term and "wants" varieties. If you refer back to your MAP, you'll know how much of the check should be assigned to what area.

Start on your list of expense accounts for your spending plan.

Make it Automatic
Plan how you are going to allocate every dollar that you earn and put it to work for you. This is important, as it will help you achieve your goals and fulfill your everyday needs and financial responsibilities. It's all about organizing your monthly expenses based on your income.

Factors that you need to take into consideration include:

- **Fixed expenses:** these are expenses that are the same every month such as rent, insurance, or a car payment.

- **Variable expenses**: these are expenses that occur regularly; however, they can vary each month, based on personal use (e.g., clothes or cell phone bill).

- **Incidental expenses**: expenses that happen occasionally like gifts or travel expenses.

- **Needs:** An obligation or a necessity that must be met, such as food, rent, or medical expenses.
- **Wants:** To have a strong desire for something, such as clothes, electronic gadgets, or a food craving.
- **Cash Flow:** cash flow checking account that includes groceries, recreational (movies, dining out, hair cuts, etc). This is the only one that you watch all the time and have some "play" room in.
- **Savings:** Money for investments that will eventually replace the income you now earn by working (separate account).

The Bank Accounts :				
Cash Flow Checking Account	FIXED payments	VARIABLE expenses	Incidental	Savings
Groceries	Mortgage	Dental		
Essential Clothing	Car	Phone		
Hygiene		Health Care		
	Car Insurance	Utilities		
	Insurance	Dry Cleaning		

You can keep track of your expenses and create a more realistic MAP by dividing your bank account and assigning the accounts as follows:

Think of these accounts as separate from each other. Most banks will allow you to create sub-accounts within your main chequing account. Each bank has a different name for this system. For example, your account might be Chequing #6613 with S1, S2, and S3 as the sub-accounts. For better success, get a different account number for the savings—make it hard to access and minimize temptation by putting it in a different bank entirely. Make it a savings ONLY account, and don't get a bank card for it. That way, you'll never pull money out of your savings account on impulse.

Reality Check

Review and evaluate your financial plan—does it match up with your paycheck planner? When you use the Financial Tool Kit, you keep more of the money you already make, rather than living on the expectation of money you haven't earned yet.

Remember, you can't have it all NOW and expect healthy finances.

"It's a kind of spiritual snobbery that makes people think they can be happy without money." ~ Albert Camus

The Healthy Money Cycle

Audits, Easy as 1, 2, 3

There are two forms of audits:

- A **daily** "mini" audit, that ensures you have accounted for all the day's expenditures.
- A **monthly** audit, where you examine the balance in each of your bank accounts, tally up the month's income and expenses, and so on.

These audits are an important step in your new financial strategy. This is the simplest way to review where your money goes each month and the daily "mini-audit" saves a lot of time at month's end.

Within a few paycheck cycles it will become second nature. If you have a spouse, do your daily audit together. Dealing with money will soon become quality time for the two of you, rather than the cause of stress and arguments. Have fun, as this little audit and the other actions you take will make your dreams a reality.

Earlier, you reviewed and determined your income. You then separated your expenses, assigning monthly amount for each category.

Your new, well-paid job as bill collector:

- From this moment on, you will get and keep a receipt for EVERYTHING you buy, big or small (if you don't like the work, collect fewer receipts by spending less).
- At day's end, each amount is entered into the assigned category.
- At month's end, add up your expenses. Some will be over the assigned amount and others will be under it. As you keep track of your spending, the necessary adjustments will be obvious.

- Your adjustments have to be reasonable—you can't expect your landlord to suddenly give you a rent break!
- Don't forget that the small things add up very quickly, so make sure that you keep track of all your small expenses.

Compare

Planning and auditing your expenses will reveal your priorities and your spending habits. Compare your anticipated expenses and your actual expenses. Armed with this information, you will be able to make changes on a monthly basis and improve your spending habits.

Adjust

It is necessary to adjust your spending on a monthly basis, as it is almost impossible to predict all expenses in advance. It will take some time to assign the correct amount to each category.

Nothing is written in stone. If you have set aside $100/month for clothing and $50/month for hair care and find a coat that costs $120, you can move money from one category to the other—as long as you now only spend $30 on hair care!

Before you buy, you will have to ask, "Do I really want this and what are the consequences of this purchase?" You always have a choice in what and whether you buy.

Be Honest

This is the most important part of the cycle. Get to know yourself. If you wish to succeed, you must concentrate on the basic principles of truth, courage, hope, and forgiveness. Everyone has the power to succeed. All you need is the belief that you can do it.

NUTS AND BOLTS

Your Yearly Routine

Evaluate your financial goals:

- Have you made progress in achieving your financial goals this year?

- Over the past year, have your goals and dreams changed?

The Success Cycle will help you stick with your plan to spend less than you make. There are four basic steps to this system:

TRACK, AUDIT, COMPARE & ADJUST.

A LITTLE INSPIRATION

THE GOOSE WITH THE GOLDEN EGGS

One day a poor farmer found that his goose had laid an egg of pure, rich gold. Every morning, when he went to the goose's nest, he found another golden egg. He soon became very rich by selling the golden eggs. But he eventually found that the daily golden egg was not enough to satisfy his greedy desires. Thinking that he could get all of the goose's gold at once, he killed her and cut her open, only to find no gold. Having killed the goose that daily made him rich, he was soon poor again.

Chapter 12

MONEY RULES

"We live by the Golden Rule.
Those who have the gold make the rules."
Buzzie Bavasi

"Compound interest is the 8ᵗʰ wonder of the world."~ Albert Einstein

GP: "If there was only ONE thing that I could teach you, this is it: all you need to know is **PAY YOURSELF FIRST!**"

Ask Yourself
- Why should I pay myself first?
- What is compound interest?
- What is the "Rule of 72"?
- Saving is boring, and what if I do not live to age 65?

The Golden Rule

Few people get rich from their wages alone. But by paying yourself first and taking advantage of the "miracle" of compound interest (earning interest on your interest), almost anyone can reach long term financial goals. You don't need to be a math genius; all you need to do is pay yourself first and let compound interest do the rest.

> ## The Golden Rule: Pay YOURSELF first

GP: "This Golden Rule is the great secret of money management. If you ALWAYS take 10% of your income before tax and invest it in a long term growth program, your eventual wealth will surpass your wildest dreams. Even better, this 10% increases as your income increases.

If 10% seems like too much right now, begin by paying yourself 2%. You won't even notice it. Then pick a date where you up it by another 2%. Keep doing this every 3 to 6 months until you've reached 10%. By doing it gradually, you won't notice the difference or feel deprived.

If the Golden Rule of money was taught in schools and used by everyone, we would all be in much better financial shape."

GP: "Compound interest is a fact of life. The only real choice you have is whether you make compound interest work for you through savings or against you through debt."

The Power of Numbers

The Eighth Wonder of the World: Compound Interest

- Peggy and Henry are both 25 years old.
- Peggy, at 25, decides to invest $50 each month at 8% interest for 40 years.
- Henry decides to wait 20 years until he is 45, and begins investing $100 at the same rate as Peggy for the next 20 years (he invests **double** Peggy's amount for **half** the time that she does).
- They both invest the **same** amount of $24,000.
  Let's review their investments results.

at 65, Peggy has	174,550.39
at 65, Henry has	58,902.04

Difference: 115,648.35

When Henry invested his first $100, Peggy had already accumulated $29,451.02. To achieve the same result at 65, Henry would have to invest $296.34 each month for 20 years (**almost 6 times as much Peggy puts in each month**).

$300 versus $50: this is the **magic of compound interest**.

This gives real meaning to **"Time is Money."**

A Penny Saved is a Penny Earned

If you were offered $10,000 for 30 days of work, or one penny on the first day to be doubled each day over the same 30 days, which salary would you agree to? If you said yes to the penny, you'd be walking away from your 30 day job with over 5 million dollars!

The "Rule of 72"

This allows you to determine the number of years before **your money doubles**, whether in debt or investment. Here is how to do it: Divide the number 72 by the percentage rate you are paying on your debt (or earning on your investment).

Let's Play!

You started a savings account with $500 and earning 4% interest. $72 \div 4 = 18$. It will take 18 years for your $500 to double to $1,000 if you don't make any deposits.

NUTS AND BOLTS

Interest is the cost of borrowing money from a financial institution. This is referred to as "Simple Interest."

Compound interest is interest earned from reinvestment of interest.

A dollar a day invested at 10% interest becomes a million dollars in 56 years.

The Golden Rule + Compound Magic = FINANCIAL FREEDOM

A LITTLE INSPIRATION

THE MISER AND HIS GOLD

There lived a miser who buried his gold in the ground and thought of nothing else, night and day. He visited his hiding spot so often that a local lay-about guessed at his secret. Not long after, the miser visited his treasure only to find it gone. He cried out until a concerned passerby asked to know what was wrong.

"My treasure has been stolen!"

"What!" said the passerby "You buried your treasure so far from home. Wouldn't it have been better to keep it at home and then you could have used it anytime you needed it?"

"Anytime?" shouted the miser, "I never used it!"

"Well then," said the passerby, "Why don't you put a rock in your hiding hole? Since you never used the money, it will be just as useful."

Chapter 13

INVESTING VS SAVING

"Only in its usages does money take on meaning"
Aesop

"The safe way to double your money is to fold it over once and put it in your pocket." ~ Frank Hubbard

GP: "Charles, what are you doing about your retirement?"

Charles: "GP, I'm not even 20. I'm way too young to think about retirement! I'll get around to dealing with it when I'm older."

GP: "I've heard a lot of people say that. It seems like it's never convenient and there's always something more important to put money towards and then, 'suddenly,' it's too late to enjoy a wealthy retirement. And don't forget, the younger you are when you start putting aside a little something for retirement, the more the magic of compound interest will work for you!"

Do some research and learn about investing and which companies are doing well. When it comes to investing, you are the best financial planner for your future. I say this because you are the person who knows what your true goals and dreams are.

Savings are for your immediate or short term goals. You put money aside so that you can pay for planned purchases (whether wants or needs), while investment meets long term goals for retirement by generating new income to replace the money that you currently earn from your labour.

Take Some Money Back From the Tax Man (*In Canada*)
All Canadians who earn wages work for the government from January 1st to mid-June. Employees have a big portion of these taxes taken directly from their paycheck, while the self-employed must remember to set aside the portion that the government will claim. It is no surprise that many Canadians seek legal (and sometimes illegal options) to keep more of their hard earned cash.

Why cheat the tax man? You don't need to. You might be eligible for a tax deduction. **Keep ALL your receipts**, check the Revenue Canada website (www.cra-arc.gc.ca/whatsnew) for types of deductions, and ask your accountant what can be claimed.

The Government of Canada offers a wide range of measures to help Canadians save on their taxes. When filing your tax return, check to see if you can claim any of the following:

- Public Transit passes
- Text books
- Interest paid on Student Loans
- Moving expenses
- Children's physical activity program fees
- Cost of tools of trade
- Charitable & Political donations
- Medical expenses
- Pension income on behalf of a lower-income spouse.

One very good reason to file your taxes (other than the fact that it is the law) is that when you want a loan for big items such as a mortgage, the lender will ask to see the last two years of your income declaration as verified by Revenue Canada.

Registered Retirement Savings Plans (RRSPs)

Plan for the future and reduce your taxes. Since 1991, RRSP contributions can be deferred. This sounds great, but the reality is that it is not a good idea because you may never "catch up" and you lose the earnings that compound interest would be making for you. With our tendency to put off financially responsible decisions to tomorrow, we often forget that time is money.

The first thing you should do is to get your employer to deduct your *pay yourself first* money from your paycheck and transfer it directly into a long term investment fund or RRSP. By making this a payroll deduction, the income tax taken from your pay will be reduced.

The government wants to encourage retirement savings in Canadians. When you buy RRSPs, you defer the income tax you owe on that money until such time as you pull the money out of the program. Presumably, you'll be earning less when you retire, so you won't have to pay as much tax, if any, on it. By contributing to RRSPs through a schedule of regular payroll deductions, you realize the tax savings immediately as you will be taxed on the difference.

The average Canadian wage earner would see a $350 tax savings for each $1000 they put into an RRSP.

Let Play!

Let's assume you are earning $50,000 per year and decide to bring your lunch, saving $5 a day, 250 days x $5 a day = $1250 per year after taxes. At a 30% tax rate, that's the same as a raise of $1786 per year or 3.6%.

For a person with a marginal tax bracket of 40%, this means that an investment of $1000 in an RRSP will give back $400 in taxes.

RRSP contributions make a good investment if you want to benefit today as well as plan for your future. Deductions are based on the marginal tax bracket, or the amount of tax paid on the last dollar of earned income.

Registered Education Savings Plan (RESP)

The cost of college and university education is high and getting pricier by the year. If you start saving for your children's education at a young age, you can benefit from compound interest. Currently, the government will match your RESP savings by 20%, up to $400 a year until your child turns 16.

Start Your Own Business

Many deductions are available for small businesses (even part time). If you are willing to put in a great deal of time and effort for five years (on average), the reward of a business will be the best investment you will ever make.

A word of caution! Before you jump head first into starting your own business: ***DO YOUR HOME WORK***

Make a point of researching your market, the competition, associated costs, have a business plan, etc.

Emergency Funds

A healthy emergency fund should cover 3 to 6 months of current expenses or your gross salary. For example, if you earn $20,000 a year, you should have an emergency fund of $5,000 to $10,000.

You can quickly calculate how many days you can survive without an income right now:

- Add up your liquid assets (money in bank, or anything you can quickly sell).

- Divide your liquid asset total by your yearly expenses and then divide that by 365.

NUTS AND BOLTS

Many people don't realize that there are advantages right NOW to putting money into an RRSP plan.

- You can reap some of the benefits now!

- You defer paying taxes until you are in a lower income bracket.

- Your RRSP contribution may put you into a lower tax bracket, in which case you pay less tax.

As part of creating a life without financial worry, make the following commitment to yourself:

This year, thanks to my financial management plan, I will:

Deposit _____ in my RRSP.

Reduce my debt by _____.

Build my emergency fund to _____.

A LITTLE INSPIRATION

A DEER BY THE FOREST

A deer that lived in a forest by the sea had the misfortune to lose the sight in one of her eyes. From then on she grazed by the shore of the sea, her good eye turned towards the forest on the assumption that any danger would come from the woods. One day, a boatload of hungry fishermen passed by the deer's favorite meadow. She was promptly shot and cooked. The clever deer had forgotten that we cannot foresee all possibilities.

Chapter 14

PROTECTION FROM THE STORM

"We cannot prevent the unexpected."
Aesop

"In order to do what really matters to you, you have to, first of all, know what really matters to you." ~ Dr. Ed Hallowell

GP: "Charles, I've taught you what I know about managing money for yourself so far. But what about looking after the people you love? Do you have insurance or a will? Does your will say whether you want to be buried or cremated? Or what kind of service you want? These decisions have financial as well as emotional impact on the people you leave behind."

Charles: "GP, Why would I need insurance?"

GP: "Well, we buried your cousin Patrick on his 19th birthday. Do you think for a minute that we ever thought we'd have to do such a terrible thing? He was driving home from work, looking forward to dinner, when his brakes failed. He crashed into a bridge pillar and died immediately."

Charles: "Yes. Patrick was an amazing guy."

GP: "At the wake his boss told me how Patrick got his job. It required constant heavy lifting and Patrick wasn't exactly muscle bound. His boss wasn't sure about hiring him because he didn't look up to the physical demands of the job, Patrick said he'd give him a trial week's worth of work. After three days, Patrick's boss offered him a permanent job. His boss said Patrick was the best employee he'd ever had.

But there was one piece of "heavy lifting" that poor Patrick failed to do. He didn't have a will or life insurance. Like you, he couldn't imagine ever needing it. Did you know a funeral costs almost $10,000? Do you think Patrick wanted his mom and dad to scramble to come up with the money for his funeral in the middle of the most terrible grief a parent can know? Of course not! "

Making it Right for those I Love

Another vital aspect of financial manageability is taking care of the people you love. If you didn't make it home for dinner tomorrow night, would your family be okay, financially? Or would they be grieving for you with the added stress of losing their home, making tuition payments, paying off the credit cards and leases, trying to meet the monthly bills, cover funeral costs, and so forth? Even if you are single, your parents or siblings will have to cover the cost of a funeral.

GP: "No matter your age, if you have people you love, you should have a will and some form of insurance policy. The unexpected can happen, Charles. I miss my son and my grandson so very much, and they were both taken away before they ever had much of a chance to live.

Charles, what if you had an accident that didn't kill you but disabled you?

You would be alive, yet unable to earn an income and requiring care at an extra financial cost to your loved ones. Do you want your parents to spend their retirement savings looking after you? Do you want money that you and your spouse have set aside for future goals to disappear, when a little advance planning will ensure that the only grief your family feels is for you, and not the stress of looming financial disaster? Insurance and an up-to-date will should be part of your financial plan."

To figure out how much insurance you need, you have to ask yourself the right questions:

- What do I have (assets and liabilities)?
- Who do I want my insurance to protect?
- How much do I need to make sure my loved ones won't suffer financially?

When you have answered these questions, you will have the knowledge to get just the right amount of insurance, rather than being under or oversold on a policy by an insurer.

Whole Life policy vs. Term policy—Compare the Results

Sylvie and Peter both 25 years old, buy a $125,000 life insurance policy.

Sylvie's $125,000 Whole Life policy costs her $100 a month, pays 4.2% interest, and will mature in 40 years.

Peter decides to get a $125,000 Term Life policy. The fees are only $7 a month, and he invests the other $93 dollars a month for 40 years with a 12% rate of return.

If case Sylvie or Peter dies early, their heirs each get the same $125,000. But if they make it to retirement, here's the difference:

> Peter's monthly investment of the extra $93 has turned into a substantial $700,000.

> Sylvie's monthly premium of $100 only returns $125,716.

> Term insurance costs much less, yields a higher payout at death, and you can use the money saved on premium costs to invest and build wealth.

The Hen that Laid Golden Eggs

You are the lucky owner of a hen that lays $40,000 worth of golden eggs every year. Unfortunately, there is a 25% chance that the hen will be unable to produce eggs for one year or longer. What to do? Disability Insurance will provide you with a replacement income until your hen can start laying those golden eggs again.

In real life, you are the one that brings home that $40,000. And you have a 1 in 4 chance of being unable to work for a year or more during your working lifetime. So it is important to have enough disability insurance to ensure that you'll be able to pay your bills, mortgage, and all the other things your wages currently cover.

Insurance at a Glance

A word of caution—always read your insurance contract very carefully. Make sure you report your medical conditions accurately, as errors mean that the insurance company will not pay out the benefit. Antiques, jewelry, or a classic car may need additional insurance. Keep in mind that there are many types of insurance out there, so keep looking till you find one that best suits your situation and needs.

NUTS AND BOLTS

- *Life Insurance*—pays out a lump sump to your heirs if you die.
- *Group/Employee Life Insurance*—same as above, but do you know what happens if you leave your job? Is this insurance renewable or convertible? It is important to review the options and costs.
- *Disability Insurance*—covers you if illness or injury prevents you from working.
- *Mortgage Insurance*—pays off your mortgage in the event of your death.
- *Home Insurance*—protects against fire, theft, and other disasters. If your home has been going up in value, does your insurance reflect this in case you need to replace it after a fire?
- *Car Insurance*—protects you in the event of accident and theft.

This is your family's future and it is in your hands.

"I wanted a perfect ending. Now I've learned, the hard way, that some poems don't rhyme, and some stories don't have a clear beginning, middle, and end. Life is about not knowing, having to change, taking the moment and making the best of it, without knowing what's going to happen next." ~ Gilda Radner

GP: "Charles, did you know that fewer than 40% of Canadians have a current will? It is very important to have a will to direct your last wishes so that the people you want to look after are not embroiled in legal problems."

Wills

Unexpected things come up—so try to make the best of it by being prepared. Review your will every five years (sooner, if your life situation changes—marriage, divorce, remarriage, children, deaths, significant changes in assets, etc.). Keep in mind that divorce or annulment does not necessarily revoke your will. A copy should be kept by you and a second copy should be left with your executor.

Dying Intestate

- If you are intestate (without a will) at death, your possessions will be distributed as per the Civil Code.
- If your will is not kept up to date, and your beneficiary predeceases you, your estate will not be distributed according to your last wishes.

HOW TO WRITE A LEGAL WILL

(This Will must be hand written)

> THIS IS MY LAST WILL and TESTAMENT.
>
> I, the undersigned, (last name, first name, social insurance number) being of sound mind and memory declare this to be my last WILL and TESTAMENT.
>
> I revoke all prior Wills and Testaments at any time heretofore made by me.
>
> I give and bequeath (determine beneficiaries and property).
>
> I appoint _____ as Executor of my Will.
>
> Signed and dated at [City and Province] on this ___ day of _____, 20___
>
> Your signature

NUTS AND BOLTS

Depending on where you live, a handwritten (or holographic) Will may not be considered legally binding, although it is usually given some consideration. Check your provincial or state laws regarding what constitutes a legal Will.

Standardized Wills can be inexpensively purchased from book and stationery stores.

A LITTLE INSPIRATION

Monique Amyot & Leo Lafreniere  Founders of the Bear Hug

Together Everyone Accomplishes Miracle

"I wish my arms could reach across the miles and give you a great, big HUG!

One night, I woke up and sat down at my desk and drew a picture of a little bear giving a hug (I can't draw!). My daughter's best friend was losing her brave battle with cancer. This triggered thoughts of the wonderful friends that I have also lost to cancer and my little inner voice urged me to do something.

Family and friends, students and community members committed themselves to heightening public awareness and raising funds for cancer research and patient care. For a year, we hosted all sorts of fundraising events.

We were to mark the end of our fundraising by holding a huge Bear Hug around the Ottawa Canal. Less than two months before it was due to happen, a logistical issue destroyed a full year of hard work and preparation. That is when the miracle of giving took place. A student counselor from one of the participating schools stepped forward and took on the challenge of making the Bear Hug happen at his school. The student body, teachers, and administration helped to meet the tight deadline. They were galvanized by the fact that one of their own students was currently battling cancer. The event was a great success breaking the Guinness World record and donating $108,000 for Cancer Research and patient care.

Four years later the T.E.A.M created a 2nd record-making Bear Hug that spanned both sides of the Rideau Canal, from Laurier Street to the Pretoria Bridge. That day, many of us smiled through tears as we hugged, remembering the friends and loved ones we had lost. Thanks to the spirit and dedication of the 11,000 students committed to discovering a Cure for Cancer, we also raised three times more money than at the first Bear Hug!

Born of my desire to give something back, the Bear Hug project succeeded in uniting a whole community while providing it with hope, love, and inspiration.

May this event continue helping to save lives and find a cure!"

Monique Amyot

Chapter 15

GIVING BACK

"You have not lived a perfect day, even though you have earned your money, unless you have done something for someone who will never be able to repay you."
Ruth Smeltzer

"Happiness is not in the mere possession of money; it lies in the joy of achievement, in the thrill of creative effort." ~ Franklin D. Roosevelt

GP: "Charles, I made sure that all my children had the opportunity to get a good education. These days especially, the right education makes it much easier to get a good job, to become a valued employee, and to be in the happy situation of having money for your wants, as well as your needs. You work, you make money, and you spend the money you HAVE, not the money you plan on having!

I believe that, no matter what happens in my life, I am responsible for the results. Everything is possible. You just need to visualize your dreams and convert them into GOALS."

The Gift of Responsibility

We live in a culture of instant gratification. While there are many benefits from today's technology and convenience, I believe our children are missing important lessons that guided previous generations into maturity. Do your children know what it is to want something, to earn and to save for it, and to overcome obstacles along the way to achieve their desired dream?

GP: "You teach best that which you have the most need to learn. Once you make a decision to break your own cycle of financial unmanageability, you will have the skills and knowledge to teach your children how to have productive and profitable relationships with money.

Parents who gratify a child's every wish give short term pleasure—but it is at the expense of long term pain. A few short years later, these children become easy targets for the debt monster. They lack the understanding that satisfying a current whim will result in anxiety and depression as they struggle to meet the financial obligations created by undisciplined spending."

Responsibility to Children

Parents have become too concerned with leaving financial wealth to their children. But it is not the material goods that you leave to your children that matter most; what you leave inside them this is the true wealth. Your job as a parent is to teach your child how to survive, to be responsible, and to make wise choices in life.

Giving or Receiving – What's the Difference?

There is nothing better than to give to those we love.

Have you ever noticed the feeling of joy you feel when you offer a gift to a loved one? Or the sense of satisfaction you get when offering a donation to an organization that will make a difference in someone's life?

Remember that a sincere donation will never impoverish you nor will keeping all your possessions make you rich. One of the best feelings comes when you are in control of your money and realize that you have funds to help the people you love and support the causes that you believe in. If you can also give time, energy and understanding, your donation will go even further.

GP: "Once you master money, it is your responsibility to teach your kids as well.

Charles, I know I've taught you how to fix cars, and I hope that you have also learned this:

- Money is a tool. It should be your servant, not your master.
- Use your dreams to motivate your financial habits.
- Always pay yourself first.
- PLAN for your needs and wants, and you will avoid the debt trap.
- Follow the road to financial freedom by not letting possessions own you.
- Be a role model—show your friends and family how to live well and how to give back."

What Do You Expect from Your Money?

The real power of financial well-being lies in a state of limitless emotional grace. Because you are in the habit of being responsible and no longer spend time in a cloud of financial anxiety, you can be truly generous with your kindness, your love, and your knowledge.

You have reached the ultimate financial freedom when:

- You know without a doubt that you have done all that is possible to ensure the security of your family.
- Money is plentiful and available for your needs and your dreams.
- Money is simply a support and not who you are, or your primary focus.

If you apply what you have learned about understanding the value of money and taking charge of your finances, you will achieve financial freedom. Make the decision each day to keep your dreams in mind and be conscious as to whether your daily spending and saving decisions are moving you towards or away from them.

You owe it to yourself and your loved ones to drop the burdens of the past. Your old money attitudes and behaviors are too costly and keep you from living a life of happiness, security, and generosity.

A HAPPY ENDING

GP: "Jane and Joe came to my garage to get their car brake replaced. They were worried about how they were going to pay, as they made below average income and had two young daughters. I remember they both looked tired and rundown. I asked them if they had a budget. They did, but they kept fighting over it because the numbers never worked out at the end of the month because there were always surprises (like the brake job).

I knew how they felt, because I had tried the same thing a few years ago and it hadn't worked, either. So I asked them if they had been taught the secret of the Golden Rule. I explained that they had the choice of continuing to live paycheck to paycheck, like almost everyone else, or they could learn how money works and enjoy a stress free life!

The secret is very simple. Every time you earn a dollar you must pay yourself first. Most people are taught that they have to pay their bills first, and then try to budget for emergencies, retirement, and big ticket items. But there is never enough left at the end of the month to do this. To make a long story short, Joe and Jane tossed their budget and started to pay themselves first.

Twenty-six years later, Joe and Jane came back for a visit to my garage. They came in holding hands, laughing, and with the spark of a young couple in love. Joe had just retired, at only 52. They had been able to pay their girls' way through university and both daughters were doing well.

Joe and Jane had bought the old house they were renting, had fixed it up and, when they bought a newer house some years later, held on to the first one and rented it out. Joe had asked his boss to take 2% of his gross paycheck off every week and put into the company pension plan. That was so easy, that he gradually increased the deduction by a few percentage points until 10% was being put into investments. And, with the magic of compound interest, the money started to pile up. They had also followed another important money sanity rule: **Live on cash, not credit.**"

Imagine the Life of Your Dreams

- How does money apply to my dreams?
- What do I *really* want?
- What the does my mind have to do with money?
- Why should I change?

A Clear Road to Success

Live a life that has clear and precise goals and have the courage to realize them. Remember along the way to always see the beauty in all living things. Today is a gift, so concentrate today's direction towards your DREAMS.

- Believe that what you have now is the best and that you do have the control to change the future.
- Believe in yourself & CHOOSE to BE HAPPY every day of your life, regardless of the obstacles.
- Commit to daily improvement; challenge yourself to be better.

Become aware and start using the Financial Tool Kit:

- What's your PLAN?
- Take a Financial SNAPSHOT.
- Create your money management MAP.

A good money management plan is like eating right, rather than going on a diet. Smart money use is healthier than extreme cutbacks and doing without, but you still need to know where your money is going.

GP recommends tracking your living costs in categories like those on the CD's *Expense Tracker*, or entering the information in personal finance software (like Quicken or Money), and asking yourself questions similar to the following while reviewing the reports each month:

- Where is our money going?
- Do we really need to put so much into this category?
- We spent more than expected in this category this month. Why? And what can we do to prevent it from happening again?

For additional information, please visit *www.solutionfinance.ca*. If you are looking for a financial advisor, educator, or coach who understands the Personal system and would like contact information, please to go to *Resources* (page 145) and find the resource most suited to your needs.

SECTION THREE

YOUR 30 DAY PLAN

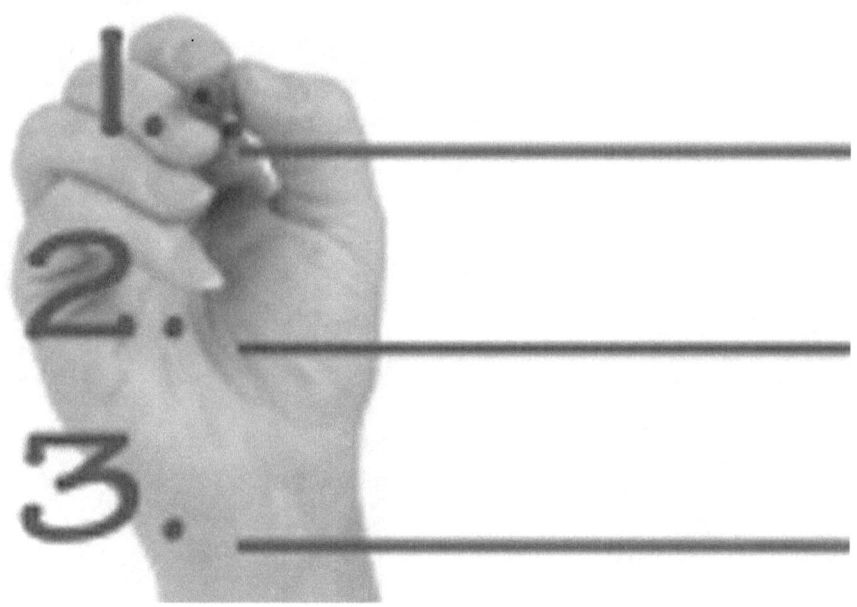

"The best place to start is where you are with what you have"

Charles Schwab

Starting Now

Follow this 30 Day Plan and you are guaranteed to succeed. It will give you the practical experience necessary to create new financial habits—ones that work for you instead of against you! From reading *Who Took My Money?* you should now understand much more about your attitudes and habits towards spending, debt, and savings; you can see how they keep you from enjoying financial happiness and are committed to making some simple changes.

The 30 Day Plan is the next step of your journey. It's time to put the lessons learned into practice. On the included CD you will find the sheet needed to perform your weekly tasks. Set a time in your agenda and commit to action. Once you see how it changes your life for a better financial well-being, why would you want to go back to your old ways? Give it a try; it's worth the trip!

Perform the following exercise:
I will be happy with my money skills when .... (complete the sentence).

The price I MUST be prepared to pay:
I am willing to .... in order to reach my definition of satisfaction (complete the sentence).

Tell Yourself:

- I commit to do things differently today.
- I commit to change to be free of debt.
- I will always allocate enough money from my paycheck to meet my needs.

You must maintain responsibility for your relationship with money.

- Money does not ensure happiness, but how do I feel about myself?
- What impact does financial freedom have on my happiness?
- How does money apply to my dreams?
- What do I *really* want?
- What does the mind have to do with money?

- Do I value peace of mind?
- Why should I change?

As part of creating a life without financial worry, make the following commitment to yourself:

This year, thanks to my financial management plan, I will:
- Reduce my debt by _____.
- Build my emergency fund to _____.
- Deposit _____ in my in my investment account.

The future is your responsibility and you can make it FUN!

BEGIN A FINANCIAL JOURNAL TODAY

Start a journal in which, every time you spend money, you write down *what* you spent, *why* you spent it, *whether* it was planned or unplanned, and what emotions you experienced at the time. You should also write down how you feel about beginning this program; does it feel good, is there fear, anger, self-pity, resentment, satisfaction, empowerment, relief, hope, and so forth? Note the changes you make to aid your goal of financial fitness and the times when old habits take over.

Your journal can be electronic or on paper. Don't worry about spelling or making sense. The Financial Journal is a very important tool in your battle to become aware and have power over money instead of letting it control you! My experience is that everyone who keeps a daily Financial Journal succeeds in meeting their money goals. In particular, it's great for emotional spenders but it works for everyone.

MAKE YOUR FINANCES A FAMILY AFFAIR
Together Everyone Accomplishes Miracles

Have a good talk with your spouse and children; everyone should be involved. Planning your financial well-being is the longest trip you will ever make. To avoid traveling on bumpy roads and to assure that you plan to succeed, the entire family should participate.

Little task: Today, as a TEAM, you will find a piggy bank. Be creative, there is no need to buy anything.

Be Honest: Practice self-awareness. Whether you are single or part of a family, you will have to focus on the essential principles of truth, love, courage, hope, and forgiveness in order to successfully change the old behaviours that are a barrier to financial success. If you believe, you can do it.

Week 1

The first week is the hardest. You need a boost. Just like starting a new sport—it feels uncomfortable and stressful at first and then the more you practice, the easier it gets. Learning how to manage your money is no different. Make it fun!

This week restrict yourself to shopping for **needs** only (like groceries) and **pay only with cash**.

- Set times for this week's tasks.

Become aware and start using the **Financial Tool Kit:**
- Create a Dream Board.
- Take a Financial SNAPSHOT.
- Set up your MAP.
- Open new Bank Accounts.
- Get Organized (filing).
- Commit to Debt Elimination.

DREAM BOARD

Have fun creating your Dream Board. Set the financial components of your dreams as goals. *Use the CD's Goal Setting worksheet.*

Imagine!
You are walking on the beach and suddenly you see a little bottle. You open it and the genie says: "Your wishes are my command." What would your wishes be? Put them in writing.

SNAPSHOT

What is your current net worth? Calculating your net worth is fairly simple. *Use the CD's Net Worth worksheet.*

Am I rich or poor? Let's see!

Know where you stand financially today.
• Take this time to create your snapshot

MAP

Track your living costs in categories . *Use the CD'S Expense Tracker worksheet.*

You may prefer to enter the information into your personal finance software like Quicken or Money.

Go on a treasure hunt to find a few bank statements and see what your actual obligations are. Create broad categories into which you will allocate the amounts, as close to reality as possible.

Some of these categories will be cash (groceries, entertainment, walking around money, clothing), while others should remain electronic (housing, investment, savings, utilities, debt repayment, health). Transportation, for example, might have an electronic component— insurance, loan/lease payments—and a cash component—gas, taxis, bus fare.

Find a song in your music collection that will become your theme song. My favorite one for this is: "I Want Money" by the Galloways.

For the cash categories, label some jars with names and the amount of cash to be put into them each week.

CASH ONLY (It's Worth a Try)

This week, you won't use your credit card or debit card to purchase anything. All your spending will be done with cash.

Each morning you will only take enough cash to get through the day's planned activities. All the plastic cards and the checkbook stay at home (in the vault)! You will be amazed at how the unconscious spending habits that are so much part of our normal day add up when you are parting with cold cash.

> **TIP:** When you take out your cash for the week, ask the teller for seven $5 bills. Fold each bill lengthwise and then lay them against each other and put them in your wallet. This is your gum and coffee money for the week. Be conscious of how it feels to pull out each bill and how the emotions you experience as you reach the end of your "bill-fold."

At first, you may run out of money before the week is over, but it usually isn't long until there is money left in each of the discretionary spending categories.

NEW BANK ACCOUNTS
Make it easy. You will want to create bank accounts and automaticize your payment (see page 97).

Many banks will allow you to create subsidiary bank accounts attached to your main account. If your bank doesn't allow this, find one that does.

You can keep track of your expenses and create a more realistic MAP by dividing your bank account and assigning the accounts as follows (see page 98):

- **Cash Flow:** chequing account.
- **Needs:** a necessity that must be met like food.
- **Fixed expenses:** The same amount every month.

Make arrangement to have all bills paid **automatically**. Once this is done, you will have more time for fun.

- **Variable expenses:** These occur regularly and may vary monthly. Most bills can also be paid automatically, but you need to make sure that there is always enough money to cover the incoming payments.
- **Incidental expenses:** Occasionally expenses.
  This category is like a mini-saving account for the stuff you will want in the near future, such as Christmas gifts.

- **Savings:** for short term goals (open a different account) such as a vacation, new couch, etc.
- **Wants:** a strong desire for something.

It's Payday

Deposit into each account the amount required. For the cash categories, make a weekly trip to the bank and pull out the exact amount of money you need to fill each jar.

ORGANIZE

Create a filing system (see page 80) for each of your categories and put receipts, bills, invoices, pay slips, RRSP updates, etc. in the relevant files at the end of each day as they come in.

Become a bill collector. Keep ALL receipts and if you don't like the work collect fewer by cutting the little expenses. The small expenses are often the reason why your money runs out before the next paycheck.

DEBT ELIMINATION

Your strategic repayment plan (see page 47). *Use the CD'S Debt Elimination worksheet.*

Remember, if you are just meeting your minimum payments it could take decades and thousands of dollars in interest to pay off your debts.

Congratulations! You made it through this 1st week!

Now, reward yourself. You've saved, so spend a little; bring home a bottle of nice wine or some flowers; treat the family to pizza. The money spent should come from an overflow from one of your accounts or jars.

> Once you have completed Week 1's task list, you can achieve any money goal you want with a commitment of only 10 to 15 minutes a day.

Week 2

This week you'll continue to build awareness and healthy money habits so that you can map out your financial directions.

This week's tasks are:
- Review your financial journal
- Start Reading
- Reassign
- To-Do List Completion
- Ongoing Tasks

REVIEW

Look at what you wrote in your journal to see what feelings were associated with specific money activities. Can you identify any emotional patterns attached to certain spending habits? Does it reveal any of the danger signs that lead to overspending?

Using your Dream Board and the review of your Financial Journal, map out how your spending, savings, and investments are lining up with the financial goals that are part of realizing your dreams.

READ

Start reading the additional materials. *Use the CD's Reading folder and choose a topic of your choice.*

I encourage you to read some additional financial management books—*The Wealthy Barber* by Roy Chilton is a classic investment manual for a good reason! One of the best basic money books that I have read is *The Richest Man in Babylon* by George S. Clason.

Allocate some time each day for new reading material. You will soon cherish this new habit.

REASSIGN

Each week, you may need to reassign money from one category to another. For example, if your heating bill is higher than expected, you might decide to invite your friends over for popcorn and a movie on the weekend, rather than a night on the town. Move the money saved from your chequing account into your Variable account to pay for the extra amount of the utility bill.

Now that you have committed to spending only money you actually have, you will need to make choices that involve spending less in one category when more is spent in another! Overspend on your walking around money and you have to find the money in another category.

See the CD's **Saving Tips Folder** for different ways to cut expenses. For example, if you find you are spending too much on groceries look at the sheet called GROCERIES

TO-DO LIST COMPLETION

Make a list of anything on the Week 1 Task List that you still need to do. Then do it promptly!

If you aren't finishing your tasks because they seem too scary, you feel too tired, they're too hard, or you don't have the time, ask yourself this:

- How much time do I spend worrying about money right now?
- How much fear do I have when the bills arrive or when I think realistically about my future?
- How good would it feel to know that I have money in the bank to pay my bills?
- Do I want to go on holiday without using my credit card?
- Do I want savings for an emergency and investments for my retirement and my kids' education?
- Do I want to feel happy and worry free when I think about my bank accounts?

ONGOING TASKS

From now on, every week, some tasks will be the same:
- Withdrawing money to put in your cash categories.
- Moving funds into the electronic accounts.
- Reassigning money from one category to another.
- Filling in your Financial Journal.
- Filing receipts, bills, invoices, etc.

Week 3

Continue to build new habits and maintain awareness of your spending. Review your Ongoing Tasks

This is the week where you will turn your attention to:

- Legal Issues
- Insurance
- Taxes

LEGAL

Do you have an up-to-date Will (see page 120)?

If you don't have a Will, this is the week to:
Research online to see whether you can use a simple Will kit or if your situation is complex enough that it is best handled by a professional. *Use the CD's Will worksheet.*

If you DO have a Will, review it to make sure that it covers your current situation and is up to date.

INSURANCE

Types of insurance (see page 119). *Use the CD's Insurance worksheet.* Accidents happen; be prepared and protect your love ones.

TAXES

Review (see page 110) *See CD's Tax Man.*

Week 4

By now, you should be feeling good about taking charge of your finances. The successes you've had in your first three weeks demonstrate that financial fitness is within your grasp as long as you keep on track.

This week, you'll:
- Review your Ongoing Tasks
- Compare
- Adjust

- Review
- Change

COMPARE

- Write a report indicating the total spending amount as well as the amount left in each expenditure account.
- Compare current expenditures to foreseen expenditures in each expenditure account.

ADJUST (ongoing monthly)

It is necessary to adjust your spending (see page 100). This is done on a monthly basis, as it is almost impossible to predict all expenses in advance.

Ask yourself questions similar to the following:

- Where is our money going?
- Do we really need to invest so much on this category?
- We spent more than expected in this category this month. Why?
- What can we do to prevent it from happening again?

REVIEW (ongoing monthly)

- Make appropriate adjustments to your next monthly plan; write the amounts that still need to be paid.
- Review your plan of debt elimination and adjust accordingly.
- Allocate monthly deposits in your expenditure accounts.
- File ALL your weekly transactions.
- Take appropriate decisions concerning your expenses. For each expense ask yourself: Does this much for ___ make me/us HAPPY?

CHANGE

Have a look at your financial goals (timelines, amount allocated to achieve them, priority, etc.) to see if they still line up with your desires. After a month of money awareness and empowerment, your priorities may have changed!

Start investigating through reading, online research, and consultations, what investment plan is best suited for you (remember, investments provide an income that replaces what you earn from working through rental properties, blue-chip, dividend paying stocks, etc.).

Your 30 Day Plan is for Life

If you keep up the ongoing tasks, perform the monthly review and adjustments, and work on your debt elimination plan, you WILL become financially free.

Do a daily audit. It is the simplest way to see where your money goes and it saves a lot of time at month's end.

If you lose your way at some point in the months or years ahead, acknowledge it, figure out what triggered the unhealthy spending, and start again at Week 1.

Resources

www.truehelpfinancial.com
Free help for Canadians on how to:
> Make a will
> Reduce taxes
> Life insurance
> Invest safely for the future
> Starting a home based Business
> Cover your final expenses wisely
> Understand mortgage insurance

This site is one of the best sites that I have visited, with lots of good, free information to help you.

www.Taxtips.ca – Canada
www.wwwebtax.com – US
Good savings on income tax and more

www.equifax.ca
4190 Lougheed Highway, Suite 504, Burnaby, BC
Telephone: 1-800 465 7166
Fax: 1 514 355 8502

www.tuc.ca
Telephone 1-800-663-9980
Fax: 1-905-527-0401

Experian Credit Bureau
Fax: 1-800-644-5876
www.creditbureau.ca

Industry Canada
Online: **info@ic.gc.ca**
Telephone: 613-954-5031
Toll-free: 1-800-328-6189 (Canada) Consumer Information for Canadians

Canada Revenue Agency (Administers tax laws for Canada)
www.cra-arc.gc.ca
1-800-959-8281

Better Business Bureau
www.ccbbb.ca
Telephone: (416) 644-4936
Fax: (416) 644-4945

Debt Collection guidelines
www.bankruptcycanada.com

Credit Law Information
www.canada.gc.ca and search site with key words Credit Laws

BankruptcyAction.com - Latest Bankruptcy Statistics.

Additional Reading

Richest Man in Babylon by George S. Clason (one of the best books on money I have read)

Think and Grow Rich by Napoleon Hill

The Law of Money by Suze Orman

Mind Over Money by Eric Tyson

Rich Dad Poor Dad by Robert T. Kiyosaki

Le défi de l'argent par George Soros

The Path to Happiness and Wealth by Steve Rhode (a must read)

The Wealth Machine by John Cummuta

The Average Family Guide to Financial Freedom by Bill & Mary Tooney

Lesson in Mastery by Anthony Robbins

The Roaring 2000s Wealth Builder by Harry S. Dent, Jr.

Start in the Hole, Finish Rich by David Bach

The Millionaire Next Door by Thomas J Stanley, PhD and William D. Danko, PhD

About the Author

Monique Amyot realizes that the basic financial principles her dad taught his children are "uncommon" common sense. After moving through careers in fashion design and computer systems engineering, she began work in the financial field as a mortgage professional. Many of the clients she saw were hard-working people seeking to remortgage their homes in order to solve credit card debt. Monique often shared the wisdom she had learned from her father to help these clients change their financial approach. Eventually, these informal sessions became the course "The Power of Financial Happiness" which has helped hundreds of former participants enjoy debt-free financial security.

Monique hopes to inspire a similar change through the techniques she shares in *Who Took My Money?* She loves hearing from former clients and students who contact her to share their financial milestones— paying off a mortgage, eliminating credit card debt, saving enough money to pay for a vacation in cash, or to achieve a cherished dream.

Monique's large and close family still gathers for a weekly Sunday dinner. She enjoys spending time with her three adult children and looks forward to the day that she becomes a grandmother. Her garden is where she finds peace of mind and recharges from her busy work week. She firmly believes that a little time spent in nature reminds us of the truly important things in life. Monique has a close network of friends who know how to have a good time and enjoy life to the fullest! Her lifelong interest in fashion is represented through the unusual hobby of millinery. Monique's flattering hats are sought after by family and friends alike.

THE LEGEND OF THE BUTTERFLY

If you desire a wish to come true, you must capture a butterfly and whisper your wish to it. Since a butterfly makes no sound, it can only reveal the wish to the Great Spirit. So by making the wish and releasing the butterfly, your wish will be taken to the heavens and be granted.

Today, we have chosen to keep this tradition alive by offering you this unique butterfly in Indian celebration. Add your own silent wish, BELIEVE, it shall come true.

Spreading LOVE and HAPPINESS, one butterfly at a time

Thank you Monique, you gave us great tips and, importantly, motivated us to change our habits so that we are now on track to achieve our goals and our dreams.

—Christian

Many thanks, Monique! Your help was precious, your professionalism and quick financial help were the light at the end of the tunnel.

—Bibiane

We greatly appreciated the sound advice for those wishing to change poor spending habits and to better manage their money. Even more, you gave us back our dreams. Keep up the good work Monique

—Marie Rose & Roch

[Through] your program... we were able to rebuild our credit in a very short period of time, reduce our monthly obligations, and are now working towards building our financial future.

—Blaire & Joanne

The CD attached to the facing page contains worksheet resources, calculation tools, additional real-life stories, and other inspirational materials that will help you to achieve freedom from debt slavery and put you on the road to real wealth.

If this book does not contain a CD, or if there are any problems opening the CD, please contact us at www.solutionfinance.ca

Learn more about the path to financial happiness at
www.solutionfinance.ca